MAKE LIFE HAPPEN

MAKE LIFE HAPPEN

YOUR GUIDE TO THE BETTER RETIREMENT JOURNEY™

KEITH WILTFONG, CFP®

To my beloved wife, Deidre,

As I pen these words, I am reminded that behind every chapter, every paragraph, and every sentence, there stands a pillar of strength—you. Your belief in me, your encouragement during moments of doubt, and the countless cups of coffee that fueled late-night writing sessions have been the foundation of this endeavor.

Thank you for your unwavering support and for always being my biggest cheerleader.

With heartfelt gratitude, Keith

CONTENTS

INTRODUCTION

THE BETTER RETIREMENT JOURNEY™

In 2009, my grandfather took his last breath. He was only seventy-four years old. Having had many health scares throughout his life, we all assumed he would pull through like he had countless times before. But on February 19, 2009, God called my grandpa home.

After fifty-four years of marriage, my grandmother was heartbroken. This wasn't how she pictured the last of her days, living without him. But the pain of losing him was only the beginning, we later discovered.

My grandparents always kept their finances a secret—it was taboo back then to talk about money. Even though my father had been in the financial planning business for decades at this point, he was still left in the dark for an entire year after my grandfather's death. It wasn't until my grandmother asked to borrow money from my parents to buy us kids Christmas gifts that the truth of her financial situation began to unfold.

My grandfather—Grandpa—was a truck driver all his life. He was injured on the job in 1993. He received a severance and the option for early retirement after he could no longer work. At this time, Grandpa and Grandma had a decision to make, back when company pensions were still everyday offerings. As my grandfather signed his pension paperwork, he was given three choices: 100 percent survivorship, where my grandmother would retain the entire pension in the event of my grandfather's passing; 50 percent survivorship, where she would receive half; or 0 percent, where my grandfather's pension would die with him, but they would receive a higher monthly amount. One single check mark in a box marked 0 percent and—seventeen years later—my grandmother was left nearly destitute.

Prior to my grandfather's passing, my grandparents had three sources of monthly income in retirement: my grandmother's Social Security ($800/month), my grandfather's Social Security ($1,300/month), and his pension ($3,600/month). My grandmother was able to keep the higher of the two Social Security benefits after he died, but immediately lost the other, along with my grandfather's pension. Her monthly income plummeted from $5,700 to $1,300.

Despite this drastic decrease in income, my grandmother still wasn't quite at the poverty level—her income was a few dollars above it—so she couldn't qualify for assistance. But paying her small mortgage and purchasing groceries was a struggle. On the surface, she didn't let on. Behind the scenes, she racked up an immense amount of credit card debt, leveraged her home, and got a home equity line. Eventually, she lost the house and filed for bankruptcy. Which is when my parents stepped in.

WITHOUT A GUIDE

My grandmother is not alone. Nor was this an ignorant decision from days of old. I've worked in the financial industry for well over a decade, and every day I meet with clients on the brink of retirement who are confused, overwhelmed, and uncertain about their options. Many have met with other financial advisors and some may have a tentative plan in place, but most still wonder if it will hold up when push comes to shove.

Can I ever retire? Will I run out of money? What if the economy crashes again? Will I have to go back to work? These are just a few of the questions I hear on a daily basis from individuals and couples who have worked hard their whole lives, done all of the right things, and yet still struggle with doubt, fear, and confusion when it comes to retirement. They want assurance. They want a plan that they know will work even in the direst of circumstances. I imagine you do too.

I met with a gentleman recently who was a client at a big financial firm and unhappy with his current investment situation. While he had experienced incredible returns when the market was up, the current decline was making him sweat.

"My wife has Alzheimer's," Michael told me. "We'll have to pay for in-home care or a facility in the near future. We can't lose any more money or we won't be able to afford it."

The firm had encouraged him to be more aggressive in his investment strategy in order to earn a higher rate of return. While this advice might make sense for a healthy couple on the front end of retirement, this firm had neglected to consider important factors.

Namely, his wife's medical condition and the need for income to cover healthcare expenses in the near future. Michael wanted to ensure that his wife would be okay, especially if something were to happen to him. This was one of his top priorities, and his initial retirement plan didn't cover long-term healthcare considerations at all.

Let me explain what's happening here. Many of our clients come to us after working with another firm, and we often hear them complain that they felt like "just a number," that the firm didn't care about them, and that they were offered advice that didn't account for their unique needs or desires. This is exactly what Michael experienced with his former financial firm. And it gets to the heart of the difference between generic investment advice and a comprehensive plan.

YOUR BEST INTEREST

It's important to understand that anyone with the title "Financial Advisor" may simply be held to what is called a **suitability standard.** This means that the products they offer and sell purely need to make sense for your situation. These offerings don't necessarily have to be the best option for you; the advisor only needs to be able to justify why they are suggesting a particular path. Therefore, they'll offer packages that provide them a bigger commission despite these products being less than ideal for a particular client (and unfortunately, products that pay less commission are typically better products). That doesn't mean all financial advisors are out to get you. There are plenty of amazing financial advisors that want to and do pursue what's best for their clients, regardless of compensation.

A CERTIFIED FINANCIAL PLANNER® and anyone who holds the Series 65 (like our staff at Capstone Planning) is held to a higher, fiduciary standard. This standard requires us to do what is in the best interest of our clients, regardless of our own benefit. If I have three or four different options that make sense for your situation, I cannot—by law—sway you toward the one that provides me the biggest compensation. This means that when you work with a CFP®, you can rest assured that this person will inform you of the best option for you and point you in the right direction.

Many financial advisors focus solely on the investment portion of retirement planning, either pointing to legal liability or a lack of expertise in why they neglect other domains (like taxes, for instance). But, truthfully, this decision often comes down to profitability—a financial advisor doesn't typically make money providing tax advice so most will stick to the investment portion, where they get a lot of bang for their buck.

However, there's more to a financial retirement plan than income and investments. We have seen many scenarios unfold with our clients over the years—the premature death of a spouse, the need for long-term healthcare, the shifting of priorities, capabilities, and desires. Our clients' questions and concerns span a variety of issues such as:

- When and how should I take Social Security?
- How should I position my investments to make sure they last as long as I do?
- Am I paying too much in taxes?
- What happens if I get sick?
- What happens if I live a really long time?
- Will my money run out?
- Will my spouse be okay if I die first?
- Do I need to establish a trust?
- How do I make sure my family avoids probate court?

These are all valid concerns and ones that we should absolutely plan for, if at all possible. But you'll notice that these questions don't revolve simply around income and investments, but instead span several topics. That's because retirement financial planning is much more involved than most people think. It's also because there are many unexpected events that can threaten basic retirement plans. The bottom line is that a retirement plan should take into consideration five different financial domains: income, investment, tax, healthcare, and legacy planning. Planning for these diverse areas ensures that your retirement plan can hold up for better and for worse.

A HOLISTIC RETIREMENT PLAN

In response to this need, we created *The Better Retirement Journey*™, a comprehensive, written plan for financial success in retirement. Over the course of this book, we'll walk through every step of the journey—from creating a vision to identifying a budget to putting a plan in place for all five financial domains. Let's take a moment here to unpack why each of these fields deserves consideration and preparation:

INCOME

Without income, there is no retirement. This is the first pillar to act upon: establish where income is coming from and how much.

INVESTMENTS

Once we've established income, we dive into how current investments are structured and options for diversification. We talk about possibilities from a return-and-risk standpoint and ensure that we allocate accordingly.

TAXES

We want to educate our clients on the different taxable buckets and offer strategies to mitigate taxes not only today, but also for years to come.

HEALTHCARE

Without a plan for long-term healthcare, most people will either suffer through sickness and aging or put incredible stress on their family members, including financial stress and suffering.

LEGACY

We think of legacy a little differently than most. This is where we consider all aspects of the transfer of funds. The first consideration is the surviving spouse, to make sure that everything goes to a spouse as intended. Then we look at assets, beneficiaries, charities, and so on.

A BETTER WAY

Michael and I sat down together and walked through *The Better Retirement Journey*™ face-to-face. We discussed his retirement vision, mapped out his income streams and investments, came up with a plan for minimizing tax liabilities, identified long-term healthcare coverage for him and his wife, and set money aside that would be protected for their children. We stress-tested all of this to ensure that his wife would be taken care of in the event of his death, and that he would have plenty if he were to live longer than expected.

"Thank you," he told me after we wrapped up the planning process. "This is so much different than what I experienced before. They've been my advisors for twenty-five years, and not once has anyone sat down with me and tried to understand my situation."

This is why I do what I do—for moments like these. I love seeing our clients walk out of our doors with confidence and hope. And this isn't possible without putting in the time to understand their individual stories. Every single retiree is different, with unique needs, desires, and circumstances. It would be a shame to sell a one-size-fits-all sort of package that neglects to consider a person's vision of the future or current struggles or particular fears.

Imagine if my grandmother had sought the advice of a CERTIFIED FINANCIAL PLANNER® who truly wanted what was best for her. Imagine if she had known some of the right questions to ask—*What happens if my husband dies? What will my financial situation look like then?* Certainly she would have been spared the shame and embarrassment of filing for bankruptcy, losing her home, and asking her children to spot her for Christmas presents.

But perhaps even greater than avoiding any of these things, my grandmother would have had peace of mind. Sure, she would still be devastated by the loss of her husband. But with a plan in place, she could have stepped into that next phase of her journey with hope, peace, and assurance that she was going to be okay financially. If only she'd simply had a guide.

And that's precisely what this book is—a holistic financial roadmap for retirement—so that you can walk into this next phase with a tangible plan in place and so that you never have to face the same fear, anxiety, or uncertainty that so many others carry into this new season of life that's supposed to be enjoyable and exciting. There are worksheets included along the way to assist you on the journey and so that you have a tangible, written takeaway in your hands at the end of this book. There's no way of truly knowing that a strategy will work until you have tried and tested it. So we'll do that through different scenarios, crunching numbers and choosing the one that makes the most sense for you. This isn't a guessing game or a cross-your-fingers-and-hope-for-the-best situation.

This requires your participation: both an open mind and a willingness to put in the time. But let me tell you, it will pay off. Instead of wondering if you'll run out of money or if your spouse will be okay if you die first; instead of fearing tax increases, inflation, or economic crashes, you can enter retirement with confidence and assurance that you've considered it all. And while you may not be able to mitigate every threat, while you may not have the resources to cover every consideration, you can certainly have peace of mind that you've done all that you can to protect yourself and the ones you love.

This book is a high-level financial retirement guide that will get you started on the right path. If you're five to ten years out from retirement or already a few years in, then I encourage you to read on. This is the foundation you're looking for. If you're thirty years old and looking to start investing, this might be a good place to stop (unless of course you're helping your parents or just like this kind of stuff). It's not a get-rich-quick book. It's certainly not a comprehensive investment guide or a deep dive into taxes or IRAs or any other single topic. And it's also not ideal for those who are more than ten years down the retirement road. The advice in these pages is geared toward those that are soon-to-be or recently retired.

If you complete all of the worksheets accurately and honestly, you'll walk away with a plan—on paper—that will set you up for life, a plan that covers all five retirement worlds. One disclaimer here: life happens and things change, and therefore this plan should be flexible and fluid. But it's a starting point that's been tried and tested over the years, an infrastructure that you can update and alter as you and your plans ebb and flow.

CAPSTONE PLANNING

My grandparents didn't have a financial plan in place to guide their decisions. They didn't have an advisor they could trust to point them in the right direction. They saw a bigger monthly income check, figured they needed the extra money, and made an irreversible decision that impacted my entire family for many years to come. I was seventeen at the time, and watching my grandmother's story unfold influenced the trajectory of my life.

I began my early career in the banking industry, doing global loan syndication (a topic for another day and another book). At this time, my parents were operating their financial advising business in Florida, and they would share stories about their clients, about the positive changes they were seeing in people's lives—changes that they were a direct part of. I was intrigued. I wanted to help people, too, to make a difference in people's lives.

I decided to become a CERTIFIED FINANCIAL PLAN-NER® and join the family business, where I could bring other families my passion for education and investment along with my institutional experience. Now I own and operate my own registered investment advisory practice and have the privilege of working alongside my family and the rest of our team in our commitment to help people discover a better retirement journey.

While I'm not yet retired myself, our team has walked through retirement hundreds of times with our amazing clients—building, testing, and implementing unique plans using various strategies and mitigation techniques. Testing for the what-ifs has given me vast experience in the many facets of distribution, preservation, and legacy planning. Now, I get to bring this knowledge and experience to you.

In the following pages, you'll hear real stories and real struggles from clients that we have walked alongside. My hope is that their successes and failures will help you find your way, alleviate fear, and make informed decisions. That as I share our experiences, you'll see a clear path toward the best retirement possible. We think you deserve it.

MAKE LIFE HAPPEN

Several years ago during a morning meeting, our team discussed some of our clients who had recently embarked on extraordinary retirement adventures, trekking through South America, going on safaris in Africa, hiking the Appalachian Trail, and visiting the Egyptian pyramids. These were stories of ordinary people just like us, out there living their retirement dreams.

"Making life happen," I remarked.

We all smiled, acknowledging the truth in that statement. These individuals aren't staying at home, penny-pinching or obsessively monitoring their investments. They aren't worried about getting sick or running out of money. In fact, they're not afraid, anxious, or confused about their finances at all. These people are out there living life and doing things they love with freedom and confidence because they have a retirement plan in place that they can trust. They know their money is going to last as long as they do. They've worked hard, earned this season, and they're enjoying the ride.

That's my hope for this book—that it would be your path toward freedom, peace of mind, and confidence. That it would be your sherpa up the mountain so that you can take in the beautiful view and breathe in the fresh mountain air. So that you, too, can make life happen.

CHAPTER 1

YOUR NEW LIFE

"What do you want retirement to look like?" I asked.

Steve and Linda (not their real names) were seated across from me, eager smiles on their faces as they pictured life beyond their careers and raising children. They had earned this moment. It was time to dream big!

"Well, I'm excited to play some golf. Hang out with my buddies. Maybe do a poker night once a week," Steve said, matter-of-factly.

Linda looked at him as if he had just confessed plans to move to Sweden and become an Olympian curler. "What?" she said. "I want to go to Italy. And France! And Spain! Maybe join a wine club. You definitely won't find me playing blackjack with your boys anytime soon."

They both looked at me, sudden panic in their eyes. I smiled (and quickly put my marriage counselor hat on).

This is not an uncommon reaction to this question, at least not in my office. Most couples aren't on the same page—let alone book—when it comes to their retirement dreams. This is exactly why we start *The Better Retirement Journey*™ here. In order to map out a financial plan for retirement, we first have to identify what these years might entail. What do you want retirement to look like? Where do you want to live? What do you want to do? Where do you want to go? Who do you want to do these things with?

It can definitely be awkward when your spouse's answers differ from your own, but it's far more awkward when this lack of alignment blows up two or three years down the road because this conversation never occurred. Building this vision *with* your spouse can be fun; talking about hopes, dreams, and aspirations can be exciting and inspiring. And it sets the foundation for creating a realistic and ideal blueprint for your financial future.

THE WHY

Most clients come into our office asking the question, "Can we retire?" And I always redirect the conversation to, "Well, *why* do you want to retire?" The "can" doesn't matter until we've solidified the "why."

Believe it or not, there are a number of reasons why people retire (it isn't just hitting the magical age of sixty-five). Some people hate their job. Some people are just worn out. Some people feel like they've earned it, that they've paid their dues. Some have watched their parents work until the day they died, and they want to break this pattern. Some are forced into it—either by sickness or injuries, needing to care for loved ones, getting laid off, or a contract ending earlier than expected. While the outcome (retirement) is the same, the reasoning behind it can shift *how* you step into this season.

Identifying why you want or have to retire is the very first step in the retirement planning process. In fact, answering this question can help you determine if you truly are ready to retire. For instance, we've had several clients speak to their feelings of being overworked, but at the end of the day, they weren't quite ready to fully retire. They were ready to cut back, find more work–life balance, and travel more, and these folks went on to work part-time for several more years because they enjoyed contributing and being a part of the workforce. For those who are forced into retirement due to unforeseen circumstances, the planning process becomes an opportunity to shift perspective, gain some peace of mind, and start dreaming about the future, even if it comes sooner than expected.

Retirement should not be an emotional, spur-of-the-moment decision. When you take the time to answer the question of why, you can also determine if retirement is, in fact, the right answer. And if so, you can then take the time to plan for this monumental and exciting phase of your life.

THE SKY'S THE LIMIT

Fifty percent of people who retire end up going back to work. Think about that: half the people that retire decide that retirement is not for them. And I'll tell you that this is primarily due to boredom. Why are retirees bored? Because they never had a clear picture of what retirement would look like. They went straight from working forty-plus hours a week to having more time on their hands than they know what to do with. They were caught off guard! They thought their days would be filled with purposeful hobbies and interactions, and instead they find themselves piddling around the house wondering what to do with themselves while their spouse is off running errands again.

You see, most people don't sit down and think about the details of retirement. They might have some general ideas about how to spend their free time: golfing, traveling, watching the grandkids, or learning some new hobbies. They might fantasize about slow mornings, reading by a fire, and romantic getaways with their significant other. But will tennis and a good book fill your days for years to come? What will your social life look like after you're no longer in the office every day? What are you looking to get out of your travel experiences? And what can you actually afford?

You need to start with a plan, with putting pen to paper, and then—if applicable—sharing and discussing these plans with your significant other. At this stage, we're not thinking about a budget or mapping out costs (we'll do that in the next chapter). You're simply answering the question: What do you want retirement to look like? Here are a few important categories to consider (hint: get your pen and paper ready to jot down some ideas).

TRAVEL

Most people voice a desire to travel in retirement, either to visit exotic destinations or to make the grandchild rounds across the country. If you envision travel in your retirement future, take a moment to go one step further and identify the following:

- Where do you want to go?
- How do you want to get there (plane, train, RV, car, van)?
- Who do you want to go with (the answer is not always your spouse)?
- What do you want to get out of this trip?

Not only will answering these questions help solidify your travel destinations, but it will also help determine cost and alignment with your spouse. If you both want to travel to see different parts of the world, but your desired destinations differ, that's a much different conversation than disagreeing on mode of transportation. Jot down a few dream destinations and some details, knowing that this list will grow and change over time as you check some off and add some to it.

SOCIALIZING

The workplace provides a built-in friend group. For some, it's even like a family. In fact, you might spend more time with your coworkers than your own family members. And when you retire, those connections are suddenly gone. You will miss this (whether you think so or not). So you need a plan to replace that social interaction, whether it's scheduling more outings with friends, joining a club, or participating on a team of sorts. Some popular retirement social activities include:

- Senior center activities
- Game nights
- Meetup groups
- Parties
- Group exercise classes
- Organized trips

PHYSICAL ACTIVITY

While golf seems to be the stereotypical retirement activity, our clients participate in a variety of physical activities for a number of different reasons. Whether it's to keep up with grandkids, maintain muscle strength, socialize, or enjoy the outdoors, there's an endless list of activities that will contribute to your overall wellness if you choose to incorporate these in your daily life. Consider a few popular options:

- Walking/running/hiking
- Pickleball/tennis
- Dancing
- Bicycling/cycling
- Yoga and Pilates
- Swimming
- Team sports (like senior softball leagues or bowling)
- Yard work

CREATIVE OUTLETS

Sometimes, boredom in retirement is as simple as a lack of brain stimulation. Before racing back to the office to find a problem to solve, consider whether some other challenges can cure your lethargy. Maybe mastering a skill or engaging in an inspiring activity. Here are a few that help get the creative juices flowing:

- Cooking
- Painting/drawing
- Dancing
- Photography
- Gardening
- Writing
- Crossword/sudoku puzzles
- Knitting/sewing

VOLUNTEERING

When you're raising a family and working full-time, finding the margin to volunteer can be difficult, if not impossible. Many organizations—like Habitat for Humanity, AARP, the American Red Cross, and so on—are always looking for volunteers. Retirement is the perfect time to align your passion and purpose with your time, to continue to make an impact and feel like you are contributing in a meaningful way. Maybe you become a mentor, participate in a beach cleanup, or foster a dog. There are endless possibilities.

SPIRITUALITY

Investing in your spirituality can be as simple as spending more time in your local church, synagogue, or other place of worship. Maybe it looks like joining study groups or participating in service projects through your congregation or local nonprofits. If building homes or helping out underprivileged children in a different country is something you always wanted to explore (but never had the time to do during your working years), retirement is a great opportunity to make these dreams a reality.

EMPLOYMENT

Is there a business you always wanted to start but never had the time? A lifelong passion that you want to expand or explore? There are many reasons people seek part-time work after retirement—socialization, stimulation, supplemental income, entertainment, and more. You can be a grocery store clerk, open a bed-and-breakfast, start a consulting firm, or work at a theme park!

As you start compiling this list, be sure to give consideration to all of these areas. This is how you can establish a well-rounded picture of retirement. Don't think about how you're going to squeeze it all in—the sky's the limit. Just write down anything that sounds intriguing and we'll get to prioritization next.

TOP TEN LIST

Hopefully, you're starting to picture your life as a retiree in more detail. Now, take a moment to prioritize these activities. What are the top ten things that would make your first year of retirement spectacular? That you would look back on and be proud of checking off the list?

Here's an example from one of our clients:

1. Go on weekly date nights with my husband
2. See the Egyptian pyramids
3. Hike part of the Appalachian Trail
4. Join a book club
5. Do the weekly *NY Times* crossword puzzle
6. Host "Grandma Camp" for my grandkids in the summer
7. Take singing lessons
8. Join a ladies' cribbage game
9. Walk with my neighbor three mornings a week
10. Volunteer at the Humane Society

The moments you create in retirement are so special because you worked hard to get to where you are. It's an amazing feeling when you get to cross a couple of things off this list as those dreams become reality.

But don't worry! This is a fluid document. The only thing that is guaranteed is that *your priorities and interests will change.* Maybe you start learning how to play cribbage and discover that you actually hate card games. Maybe you go on a couple of trips abroad and find out that you would much rather travel in an RV. That's the beauty of retirement—you have time. Don't be afraid to pivot, eliminate things that don't work for you, or start all over with a new list.

ALIGNMENT

Let's circle back to Steve and Linda. After it became apparent that these two were on different pages, I invited them to come up with their Top Ten Lists. Obviously, golf and poker were among Steve's priorities, while Linda wrote France and Italy in all caps at the top of her list. None of us were surprised by the variations.

But the point of this activity is not to arrive at perfect alignment. There's no reason why Steve can't go play golf frequently without interfering with Linda's travel dreams. The goal of this activity—and why we coach both individuals to come up with their own lists—is to identify a handful of priorities and activities that define retirement for you. Discovering that your picture of retirement is different from your spouse's is an important part of the process. It allows you two to come together to create a well-rounded picture that encompasses both of your wants and needs.

International travel was obviously a priority for Linda. However, it was nowhere to be found on Steve's list. Did that mean that Linda had to set her dream aside? Certainly not. I'm happy to report that Linda goes on a couple of trips every year with a group of girlfriends that love seeing the world together. And even this paradigm is beginning to shift, as Steve has felt more grounded, less rushed, and maybe even a little bored with his weekly poker and golf commitments. He's ready to change it up!

DISCOVERY

Retirement is a new life. You've never experienced anything like it. When you were younger, you didn't have the resources or the assets to go and do what you wanted. You may have had lofty dreams and goals, but you didn't have the finances to fund these endeavors. That's why this is a constant process of evaluation, a flexible plan that changes as you get to know who you are and what you want in this new season of life.

For some, this journey does lead back to work. My dad, in his midsixties, is still in the business of financial planning. It's not that he has to do it for financial reasons, but he truly enjoys sitting down and talking with people. Having human interactions and helping people brings him happiness and contentment. We have many clients that don't envision ever fully retiring because they honestly love to work and their schedules allow them to participate in other activities that bring them joy, like traveling and socializing.

We call it the retirement *journey* for a reason. You are not done evolving as a person. You don't know how you will respond, what you will enjoy, and what you will need in this new life. Be patient and flexible as you figure it out. Think of it as a trial-and-error process, and take note of the things you want more of and the things you'd like to eliminate altogether. There is no right answer, only *your* answer.

After taking the time to discuss their visions of retirement, here's what Steve and Linda uncovered:

- They wanted to purchase a small RV and take extended trips around the US together (while maintaining their home base so that Steve could keep up with his Texas Hold'em gang and Linda could work in her garden).
- They were both tennis players and planned to take their

rackets with them on their travels, making sure the campgrounds they booked had tennis courts.

- After a few years, they also wanted to travel to Hawaii and Ireland, where they both dreamed of playing golf together.

"Anything else on the bucket list?" I asked.

Linda explained that she wanted to leave some money for their two kids when she and Steve both passed. Her parents had left her some money, and it had really helped her out in a time of need. She wanted to carry on this tradition.

Steve had a different opinion. He said, "You know, I think the kids can have whatever is left. We struggled for years and paid for their college. They're going to be fine. It's now time to take care of us."

This caught Linda's attention. She said, "Steve, I think you're right. It is time to prioritize us. It's been a long time since we made our life together—the two of us—the main focus."

By the end of the conversation, Linda was smiling lovingly at Steve. They now had a clear picture of a retirement life that they both wanted, a life they could envision together.

As an advisor, these moments are pure gold—seeing a vision come together and a couple talking about making themselves and their relationship a priority. Now, it was time to crunch some numbers. Could Steve and Linda afford to keep their house in Florida, buy a small RV, travel across the country, plan a few international trips, and maybe even set aside money to leave for their kids? There was only one way to find out: time to get the calculator out.

CHAPTER 2

PRICE TAGS

"I'm afraid we're going to run out of money," Monique said. "That's my biggest fear."

Monique and her husband, Brandon, were thirty days out from retirement and had just finalized their first-year vision. They were financially comfortable, didn't have children, and were the type of folks who wanted to see their last check bounce. They wanted to live their retirement life to the fullest. Their Top Ten List included traveling abroad each year and joining a handful of social activities.

After reading through their list, I said, "If money weren't an issue, is there anything else you'd want to do?"

They both agreed they'd spend their summers in a picturesque cabin in the Blue Ridge Mountains.

"We would love to buy a second home there," Brandon said. "But that seems like a long shot. We'd settle for renting a place every other summer."

I wrote it down on their vision list: purchase a cabin in the mountains. We couldn't give up on a dream based on an unfounded assumption.

Like so many soon-to-be-retirees that walk through our doors, Monique and Brandon's biggest question was, "What can we afford to do?" They weren't sure where to start.

Without practical tools and guidance, the process of identifying a realistic financial retirement plan was daunting at best, impossible at worst.

The truth is, there's no way to know what *is* possible without actually looking at the numbers. In other words, we have to put pen to paper, establish living expenses, estimate the cost of your retirement dreams, identify how much money is coming in, and take an honest look at any gaps. This isn't a guessing game—it's a process of testing different scenarios, exploring multiple possibilities, and making a plan that *will* work. This is the difference between walking into retirement with your fingers crossed and worry lines deepening on your face versus walking into retirement with a big, fat smile on your face.

Let's talk about how to make the latter posture a reality.

RETIREMENT BUDGET

I know most people cringe at the word "budget," and this is a perfectly normal response—no one enjoys restrictions. However, for our purposes, the intention behind building a retirement budget is not constraint, but guidance. And ultimately, freedom. We want to identify guardrails so that you can spend money on your dreams and not worry about running out.

If you consistently overspend in certain categories, you run the risk of depleting your accounts too quickly. On the other hand, if you establish practical spending patterns for each of these categories, you give yourself far more freedom to pursue all of your dreams, without fear. Without questioning if it's the right decision. This is precisely why we take the planning process so seriously—so that you can make life happen and enjoy it in the process. In this light, your budget can serve as both accountability and reassurance.

We'll start with looking at projected expenses, identifying estimated costs for various categories, including items on your Top Ten List. You'll want to include everything you can think of at this point to be as accurate as possible. However, it's likely that you'll miss something and have to add to this list as you go. You can use the previous ninety days to estimate monthly expenses and then multiply by twelve to get your annual budget.

We'll take a look at Brandon and Monique's estimated monthly and annual costs:

RETIREMENT BUDGET WORKSHEET

EXPENSE	MONTHLY	ANNUAL
Housing	$0 (home is paid off)	$0
Vehicles	$0 (cars are paid off)	$0
Taxes	$375	$4,500
Homeowner's Insurance	$150	$1,800
Food	$1,000	$12,000
Dining Out	$500	$6,000
Vacations	$1,250	$15,000
Utility/Electric	$400	$4,800
Health Insurance/Prescriptions	$1,000	$12,000
Miscellaneous/Buffer	$1,000	$12,000
TOTAL	$5,675	$68,100

(To download this worksheet, go to https://capstoneplanning.com/book)

Once you complete your budget, revisit this in ninety days to compare estimated numbers and actual expenses. Then adjust accordingly. This is something you'll want to come back to each year, taking into account that priorities and desires shift, especially as you get older.

THE RETIREMENT ARC

This projected budget reflects the first phase of retirement, or what some refer to as the Go-Go phase. Many of our clients front-load their retirement, intentionally planning to spend more in the first decade of retirement on travel and activities that require more physical strength and energy.

As they get older, motivations, energy level, and abilities change, so they plan to spend less as travel slows down and priorities shift (the Slow-Go phase). During this stage, people tend to go out less and vacations are less extravagant. Then, in later years, spending often increases when long-term healthcare costs arise (the No-Go years). All that is to say, these estimates can and will change over time, as they should. There's no way to know exactly how, when, and what these changes will look like for each person, but it's something to keep in mind as you build out a budget and think long term.

PLANNING FOR INFLATION

As you revisit your budget-planning each year, it's important to account for inflation so that you don't find yourself a decade down the road trying to live on less. If you're retired for the next twenty or thirty years, the cost of living is going to change dramatically. Think about what you paid for your home or car thirty years ago versus what you would pay now. In order to stress-test your budget and ensure that you have enough money coming in to cover expenses, planning for inflation is a big piece of the puzzle and really quite simple to do.

Historically, inflation rises by about 3 percent each year. Therefore the easiest way to plan for cost increases is to take your projected monthly costs, multiply them by .03, and add this number to your line items. These numbers might not seem significant year by year, but think about how much this adds up over two or three decades! For example, healthcare costs typically rise by 8 percent each year. When you think about budgeting and planning for long-term healthcare down the road, these numbers will likely be significantly higher when you come to need this kind of intervention. This is something important to know now so that you can plan for it, not be surprised by it, and enter this stage of life with more ease and peace of mind.

Another way to account for inflation is through an inflation buffer worksheet, which calculates ten years' of your expenses with projected inflation built in. To download the worksheet, go to https://capstoneplanning.com/book.

FROM ACCUMULATION TO DISTRIBUTION

As we discussed, retirement is like a new life. Not only do your priorities and activities change, but your spending habits change too. You've likely spent your entire adult life in accumulation mode: habitually making and saving money. When you retire, you flip a switch. You spend. You distribute this hard-earned cash. You start to see the accumulation trajectory plateau. And this can truly be terrifying.

I have a client who has millions of dollars in investments and around $500,000 in the bank, but she has stocked her home with cheap, plastic furniture. She says she can't afford anything else. After a life of pinching pennies, she can't quite figure out how to shift gears. Other clients have reached a certain level of accumulation—more than enough to live comfortably and somewhat lavishly—but if that magic number drops at all, they can't handle it. This is a difficult transition. It can take time to shift gears and change behavior patterns. Give yourself grace.

But I also want you to understand that it's okay to spend, to change directions, and to enjoy your accumulated wealth. You have to give yourself permission to let go of your attachment to a certain amount of money and to identify the experiences and things that will bring you joy in this new season of life. I can tell you from experience with many clients that continuing to hoard this money away is not the path to make life happen.

LIVING THE DREAM

After doing the math and looking at all the numbers, I sat down with Brandon and Monique the following week. "I have great news," I told them. "You can purchase that cabin in the mountains. According to your income and budget, you can easily afford it, and you'll still have some money to play with."

They looked at me, incredulous.

"Are you sure?" Monique asked.

"Wait, really?" Brandon said, chuckling.

"I'm sure," I said. "In fact, with the goals you have written down right now, you're going to have a hard time bouncing that last check! You have more than enough to purchase this home."

We went over the numbers a couple of times. This was a plan that would work. They didn't waste any time. Within ninety days, they were new owners of a picturesque mountain home. Now, they spend every summer in their own little slice of paradise. On top of that, the house has tripled in value since they bought it and is part of Brandon and Monique's healthcare plan in case they need extra cash down the road to fund long-term care costs. What seemed like a long-shot dream turned into reality and has also added layers of peace to their retirement life. This is a perfect example of *The Better Retirement Journey*™, and it all began with putting pen to paper.

For Brandon and Monique to have trusted this plan enough to start moving on the cabin in just a few days' time, they had to see a clear picture of their income—not just in that moment, but over time with many considerations. To do this, they had to test a couple of scenarios. (What if Brandon died first? What if the economy crashed again—would they run out of money?) After we created their budget, we did just this. We gathered all of their income data, tested several circumstances, and looked at the actual numbers. We didn't guess. We knew the plan would work because we had tested it.

Now it's your turn!

CHAPTER 3

INCOME PLANNING

Randy was diagnosed with a form of terminal cancer at the age of sixty-three and informed that he probably had only a few years left to live. He decided to go through with chemo and radiation to prolong his life as much as possible. He promptly retired from his job earlier than he had anticipated, took his Social Security, and committed to enjoying every second he had left—traveling, golfing, swimming, playing tennis, and spending time with loved ones.

Five years later, he was still feeling pretty great, except for the growing anxiety he felt as he watched his bank account rapidly dwindle. What would happen if those "few years" turned into a decade or more?

That's when he came to see me.

"What can I do?" he asked. "I didn't think I had a lot of time left, but I don't feel like I'm going to kick the bucket anytime soon."

"Well, maybe quit exercising so much and eating so well?" I said. "That might shorten your lifespan!"

All joking aside, Randy's story shows that even in a dire situation, in financial matters, don't plan for dying, plan for living. In Randy's case, his retired lifestyle had helped him experience better health overall. To be honest, he didn't look sick at all. The bigger problem, at least at that moment, was that he hadn't identified long-term income streams that could sustain his lifestyle. While living longer usually sounds like a good thing, it does carry risk.

If you are convinced you'll die by the age of eighty-five and plan your finances accordingly, but end up living to see one hundred, you're going to run out of disposable income.

This isn't the only risk we run up against with income planning. For instance, what if your spouse gets sick and you need to pay for long-term care? What if your spouse predeceases you—how will this affect your income? We want to make sure not only that you won't run out of money, but that you can enjoy retirement without worrying about any of these scenarios.

Randy was already a few years into an earlier-than-expected retirement, so we had to work backward a bit. But for most, you have time. Time to determine all of your income streams, and time to stress-test your plan. With this information along with the budget we determined in the previous chapter, you can determine any financial gaps and an action plan to cover those. That's exactly what we'll do over the next two chapters. First, let's take some time to gather all the information we need about your income sources.

THE THREE BUCKETS OF MONEY

BUCKET #1: SAFETY

- Description: This bucket contains funds that are 100 percent liquid and easily accessible. These are your emergency funds, savings in the bank, and other cash equivalents.
- Purpose: The primary purpose of this bucket is to provide financial security and cover unexpected expenses. It ensures that you have immediate access to cash without having to liquidate investments at an inopportune time.

BUCKET #2: INCOME

- Description: This bucket is designated for assets that generate a steady stream of income. Examples include bonds, dividend-paying stocks, rental properties, annuities, and other investments that provide regular payments.
- Purpose: The purpose of the income bucket is to provide a reliable source of income to cover living expenses, particularly during retirement or periods when you are not earning an active income. It fills the gap when your regular income streams, such as a salary, are not sufficient or have ceased.

BUCKET #3: GROWTH

- Description: This bucket includes investments aimed at growing your wealth over the long term. It can include stocks, mutual funds, high-yield securities, and other growth-oriented investments.
- Purpose: The growth bucket is intended to build and increase your wealth over time. While these investments can be more volatile, they have the potential for higher returns,

which can help you achieve long-term financial goals like retirement, purchasing a home, or funding education.

UNDERSTANDING THE DISTRIBUTION

Many people, like Randy, have an imbalanced distribution, with most of their money in the growth bucket and very little in the safety and income buckets. This can create financial instability and insecurity. Instead, each bucket needs to contain some percentage of your money to achieve the balance needed for stability and security. Remember:

- **The safety bucket** ensures you have funds readily available for emergencies and short-term needs;
- **The income bucket** provides a stable income stream, which is especially crucial for retirement planning and financial independence; and
- **The growth bucket** aims for long-term wealth accumulation, helping you stay ahead of inflation and achieve significant financial milestones.

INCOME STREAMS

The first step in building a solid foundation for our financial retirement roadmap is to identify sources of guaranteed income. The most common ones include these:

- Salary
- Pension
- IRA, 401(k), 403(b)
- Social Security
- Investment income

- Real estate/other hard assets
- Cash equivalents
- Life insurance

It's important to be open and honest as you gather this information. You might be surprised how many times I've had a client call me after an initial data-gathering meeting to tell me about a secret asset or bank account that their spouse was unaware of. You won't get very far in creating a financial retirement plan if you're hiding income streams or answering questions with inaccurate information. You should be as transparent as possible so that you can create a plan that reflects reality and is set up for success.

SALARY

For most, retirement will be twenty to thirty years of unemployment without any type of salary. If you decide to work part-time in retirement, you can account for that income in your planning process.

PENSION

In 1875, the American Express Company established the very first corporate pension plan in the US. Employees who met certain qualifications (working for the company for twenty-plus years, reaching age sixty, being recommended by a manager, being approved by the board of directors) would receive up to $500 per year upon retiring. Soon after, banking and railroad companies began offering pensions to their employees. Then large corporations joined the ranks. It was a way to keep employees around for thirty or forty years and remain loyal to the company.

By 1950, more than ten million Americans had a pension, and more and more organizations realized the value of offering a fixed post-retirement salary in exchange for years of service and dedication. And it seemed to be a win-win. Upon retirement, employees knew exactly how much they would receive each year and could plan accordingly. These set pension plans—either a fixed dollar amount or a percentage of a person's salary—became known as **defined benefits plans.**

In the 1960s, defined *contribution* plans started to make their way onto the scene. As people began living longer, companies didn't want to carry the responsibility for the rest of their lives. They wanted these employees off their balance sheets. So that's when companies started creating plans like 401(k), 403(b), employee stock ownership, and profit-sharing, where employees could make their own contributions and invest this money for later in life.

With this shift, we also started to see an automatic flow into stocks, as employees put a certain percentage of their check into the market or market-like vehicles. While defined benefit plans are still common in state and local governments, most private companies have shifted to defined contribution plans. Now, less than 10 percent of retirees receive a pension, and that number will likely continue to drop. What does this mean for us? We need to be intentional about building our own pension plan through an IRA, 401(k), or 403(b).

IRA/401(K)/403(B)

Most companies offer employees the option of making an annual contribution to a retirement plan—either a 401(k) or a 403(b)—with a built-in tax break. The company will automatically withdraw these contributions from an employee's paycheck and invest them according to this person's choosing from a list of options.

Many companies offer to match your contributions to these plans, and I always encourage my clients to take advantage of the complete match. For instance, if your employer matches the first 4 percent of your contributions, you should contribute as much as possible to maximize that additional "free money" from your employer.

An IRA (individual retirement account) is a separate account that anyone can open and contribute a certain limit to.

When you retire, you can turn your IRA, 401(k), and 403(b) into an income stream in a variety of ways—distributions, dividends, annuities, investments, and so on. And these are typically earlier sources of income, particularly because of a tax law that requires a minimum withdrawal from these accounts by the age of seventy-three or seventy-five depending on when you were born (more to come on this in Chapter 5, "Tax Planning").

SOCIAL SECURITY

If you're unclear about how Social Security is calculated or taxed, you're not alone. There are few reliable sources, aside from calling the Social Security office directly. However, while these experts on the other end of the line can give you information, it's actually against the law for them to offer you any advice.

Perhaps you've talked about Social Security with your financial advisor. Be warned: most advisors will tell you to take your Social Security as soon as possible to secure an income stream, but they often don't understand the full repercussions of this decision. In fact, taking your Social Security as soon as possible could cause you to miss out on a ton of potential income down the road.

Our team at Capstone Planning offers extensive workshops on Social Security to help people understand all of the nuances and how to calculate different scenarios. Most of our team are National Social Security Advisors, meaning we are very familiar with all the ins and outs of Social Security—the complicated rules, the hidden benefits, and how you can maximize this income stream.

With that said, let me take a moment to unravel the mystery of Social Security.

First of all, Social Security is your top thirty-five years of monthly earnings, adjusted for inflation. As of right now, you can take it as early as sixty-two or as late as seventy. After the age of seventy, there are no advantages to delaying taking your Social Security. However, there may be disadvantages to taking it too early and advantages to delaying taking it *until* the age of seventy. There are several free online resources to calculate various options for taking your Social Security at different ages.

If you ever see statements for Social Security, your full retirement age (FRA) will be noted on these statements. This number differs based on the year you were born, and it's important to know your specific age. If you take Social Security *prior* to your full retirement age, your benefits will be permanently reduced. For example, if you were born after 1960 and take Social Security at age sixty-two, you will have a 30 percent reduction in your monthly earnings *for life*. If you wait and take it at sixty-seven, you'll get 100 percent of what is called your **primary insurance amount,** or your PIA. But that's not all.

If you choose to delay taking your Social Security from your full retirement age until you turn seventy, it accrues a delayed retirement credit (or DRC) of 8 percent each year, plus whatever inflation is (if it's 5 percent, your total DRC would be 13 percent that year). Over three years, this number adds up. Simply put, if you can wait three extra years to take Social Security, you will receive over 124 percent of your PIA.

For example, for someone born in 1960, the FRA is sixty-seven. Here's how the benefits might look if they decide to start receiving them at different ages:

Early Retirement at Age Sixty-Two

If they start taking benefits at age sixty-two, they will receive a reduced amount. The reduction is approximately 30 percent for starting sixty months early (five years before FRA).

- Monthly benefit at age sixty-two: $2,000 \times (1 - 0.30) =$ **$1,400**

Full Retirement Age (FRA) at Age Sixty-Seven

If they wait until the FRA of sixty-seven, they will receive their full PIA.

- Monthly benefit at age sixty-seven: **$2,000**

Delayed Retirement Credits Up to Age Seventy

If they delay taking benefits past FRA up to age seventy, they earn delayed retirement credits. The benefit increases by 8 percent per year for each year delayed beyond FRA.

- Monthly benefit at age sixty-eight: $2,000 \times 1.08 =$ **$2,160**
- Monthly benefit at age sixty-nine: $2,000 \times 1.16 =$ **$2,320**
- Monthly benefit at age seventy: $2,000 \times 1.24 =$ **$2,480**

For our married clients, this is especially helpful to understand. One spouse can take their Social Security right away to draw some income and avoid relying entirely on investments. The other spouse can delay taking Social Security to allow this DRC to accumulate. Typically, we advise our clients to take the lower-earning spouse's Social Security first, to maximize the increased PIA. This strategy builds a solid income-stream foundation.

Furthermore, it protects a surviving spouse. When one spouse passes, the other gets the higher of the two social securities. If the higher-earning spouse waits until seventy to take their Social Security, it increases potential earnings for the surviving spouse, putting this person in a much more stable position in this unfortunate scenario.

What If I Already Took My Social Security Early?

If you've already taken your Social Security, you may still have the option of tapping into these benefits. If you've taken it within the past twelve months, you can choose to pay the money back. If it's been longer than twelve months, you can still suspend it at your full retirement age and allow it to roll up until you turn seventy (or any time before that).

Unfortunately, we have encountered a number of clients who see these numbers and say, "I really should have waited," but are out of that twelve-month window and past the age of seventy. You can't change the past, and there are other ways to establish solid income streams in retirement. For those of you on the cusp of retirement, this information can make a huge difference in your total retirement income.

YOUR SOCIAL SECURITY ACCOUNT

If you haven't already, take a moment to set up an account on ssa.gov. You can then request a Social Security statement that will list your full retirement age. You should also ensure that all of your earnings are included. If any of your former jobs are missing, collect the necessary documentation and call Social Security to make these changes. It's important that these numbers are correct, as this is the amount of money you'll receive for the rest of your life.

INVESTMENT INCOME/PAPER ASSETS

Your investment income and paper assets include all of your distributions. For each of these accounts, you will want to gather the following details:

- Account type (i.e., IRA, Roth IRA, etc.)
- Tax category (pretax, posttax, or tax-favored)
- Owner
- Beneficiaries (per stirpes or per capita)
- Current value

REAL ESTATE/HARD ASSETS

- Residential properties
- Commercial properties
- Rental properties
- Land
- Special purpose properties
- Precious metals
- Collectibles
- Commodities

CASH EQUIVALENTS

- Checking
- Savings
- Money market funds
- Certificates of deposit (CDs)
- Treasury bills

LIFE INSURANCE

The final income category to consider is your life insurance policy. Life insurance gives you access to cash value (potentially tax free), covers a spouse in the event of an unexpected death, and becomes available as a legacy for children or grandchildren. You'll want to assemble the following details regarding your life insurance policy:

- Type (whole life, guaranteed universal life, index universal life, variable universal life, or term)
- If term, remaining years
- Owner
- Beneficiaries (per stirpes or per capita)
- Current cash value (if applicable)
- Death benefit

EMERGENCY FUND

If you don't already have an emergency fund, now is a great time to create one. This is a savings account that contains enough money to cover six to twelve months of expenses or a flat dollar amount that you've identified. In retirement, this emergency fund becomes money you can pull from in an emergency—your car dies, you need a new air conditioning unit, you have a health crisis, etc.

DEBT

In order to accurately calculate income, you have to account for debt and liabilities on your personal balance sheet. This includes your home, your home line of credit, vehicles, and credit cards. You can also account for future debt here such as a new vehicle, RV, boat, vacation home, and so on. Be prepared to provide the following information:

- Owner (of debt)
- Whom you owe (company/person)
- Type (mortgage, credit card, etc.)
- Interest rate
- Monthly payment
- Duration remaining (if applicable)
- Total amount owed

SPOUSAL PLANNING

What can be done to mitigate against the risk of losing a spouse well before the expected life expectancy?

We have seen firsthand the devastating effects that *not* planning for this can have on a surviving spouse. Some decisions are irreversible, like choosing 0 percent survivorship on a pension or taking Social Security too early. While we can't go back in time, we can make sure that we fill these gaps with better assets and investments for the future.

The most obvious answer is life insurance. You can also maximize the Social Security benefit for the higher-wage-earning spouse.

On top of income, we also have to consider taxes. When you're married and file jointly, your taxes are lower. As a single person, your taxes will be a lot higher. Take the time

to calculate your income in the case of your spouse prede-
ceasing you.

IDENTIFYING GAPS

After you complete your worksheets, you'll have two estimated
totals: income and expenses. Hopefully you have a clear picture
of what's coming in and a little more confidence in the longevity
of these sources. Most often, our clients—like Brandon and
Monique—underestimate their ability to achieve their vision.
They have more money coming in than they have planned to
spend. This is a great problem to have—it simply means you
get to dream bigger! Instead of one vacation each year, maybe
you can plan for two or go even more extravagant, bringing
the whole family along on your dime. Maybe you, too, can buy
a cabin in the mountains. If this is the case, don't be afraid to
broaden your horizons.

On the other hand, sometimes the gap is the other way
around. Maybe you don't have the income to support your
vision. Maybe you've realized that your income is unreliable if
your spouse passes away first.

This is all okay. The goal is to identify these gaps as soon as
possible, ideally *before* you retire, to address them and adjust
where possible. If this is the case for you, take some time to consider various options. Some of our clients have chosen to work a
couple more years so that they can live the life they imagined in
retirement. Some have chosen to shrink their retirement vision
and reduce lifestyle expenses. Return to your budget and see if
there are ways to rework it to make retirement work. Be honest
and thorough with your considerations so that, in the end, you
have a plan that will work.

If the gap between your budget and income isn't big—say

around four or five percent of your annual budget—diversifying your investment portfolio is a viable way to fill this type of gap. Let's talk about investment planning next.

CHAPTER 4

INVESTMENT PLANNING

In 2007, just a couple of years before she planned to retire, Lori's financial advisor encouraged her to refinance her fully paid-for home and to put this money into the stock market. She trusted him, did just this, and aggressively invested $200,000.

Soon thereafter, the market went down dramatically and Lori watched as over half of her investment dwindled away. She panicked. Deciding that she couldn't take any more loss, Lori pulled the rest of her money out of investments and put it back into the bank.

Not only had Lori lost a big chunk of change, but she also had a newly acquired mortgage payment and no hope of these investments turning right side up sitting in the bank. Now, years later, she still has to work part-time to cover her expenses—one bad recommendation changed all of her retirement plans.

Let me be clear: I would never, under any circumstances, advise someone to go get a mortgage—in other words, *to go into debt*—to invest in stock. This doesn't make sense and would contradict my standards as a CFP®. My opinions aside, the deeper issue here is that Lori didn't know any better, wasn't aware of her options, and trusted her financial advisor to point her in the right direction. Unfortunately, he didn't.

Lori's story is devastating and we want to do everything we can to help you avoid these sorts of blind sides. Lori had other options that didn't involve going into debt or pulling out of the market altogether. She just needed the right guidance. This highlights one of the most important hats we wear as financial advisors, and that's the role of a behavioral coach.

It's common to feel the urge to bounce into and out of the market as it falls and rises. No one wants to lose money. However, investments are often like a bar of soap—the more you touch them, the smaller they get. And most people that pull out of the market have a difficult time getting back in. That's why it's crucial to have a diversified plan in place, that suits your risk tolerance and capacity, that can ride the waves of the market.

The purpose of this chapter is to peel back the layers on investments and truly offer a sound and tested approach on investment planning in retirement. We'll start with evaluating your risk tolerance and capacity, explain the importance of a diversified portfolio, elaborate on various investment options, and give you tools to protect against inevitable volatility. With these pillars in place, you can establish an investment portfolio that suits your unique needs, fills your income and growth buckets, and can withstand market fluctuations.

EVALUATING RISK

There are two components that we need to measure in order to determine your ideal portfolio: how you feel about risk and what you actually have to work with.

Simply put, some people are more comfortable with taking risks. Others want to play it safe. We've had a number of clients who lost substantial money in the market, pulled out, and are legitimately afraid to reenter. This is valid, and it also very much colors how much they want to invest in the future. Neither strategy—risky or safe—is right or wrong. It's really about uncovering what you feel most comfortable with and making intelligent, calculated decisions based on this intel.

RISK TOLERANCE

Our risk tolerance—meaning, how much risk we feel comfortable taking—often decreases in retirement. People are prone to risk more when they have consistent income, when they are in the accumulation mode of life. If the stock market starts to go down, it's okay because they're still working and contributing and those assets are still growing. In retirement, people lose that human capital aspect, a.k.a. the paycheck. They're more reliant on this investment capital to cover life expenses. This is why it's important to shift gears a bit in retirement—to transition to a more conservative approach, de-risk the portfolio a bit—because stock market fluctuations have a greater impact on lifestyle.

A lot of times, people are too aggressively invested. They panic and pull out because they never identified how much is too much to risk. When their investments suddenly drop 20 percent and they see an actual dollar amount attached to that percentage, they realize it's more than they ever intended to put on the line. So they jump ship, only to find that it's far more difficult to get back in the market after this experience, and their withdrawal and hesitation ultimately costs much more than that initial 20 percent loss.

This doesn't tend to happen when we take the time to determine risk tolerance. **Risk tolerance** is how you *feel* about risk. Are you okay with a 20 percent decline, which translates into $(fill in your amount)? The other element to consider here is how reliant you are on your investments. How much are you tapping into this as monthly income?

RISK CAPACITY

To determine risk capacity, we consider age, income, expenses, assets, and retirement goals to determine where you stand financially and what you need in the future. A quick questionnaire can help you identify your risk tolerance and your risk capacity. Typically, people's risk capacity is greater than their risk tolerance. Based on the results, the goal is to identify a number somewhere between these two to ensure that when the market dips, you're not tempted by emotions to pull out. You've crunched the numbers and you will be okay.

RULE OF 100

A simple tool that many advisors use to determine risk capacity is called the rule of 100. It looks like this:

$$100 - \text{your age} = \% \text{ of risky assets}$$

For instance, if I'm sixty years old, then 60 percent of my assets should be invested into safe outlets like CDs, annuities, and treasuries. The other 40 percent would be invested in more risky assets like stocks. As you get older, more of your money is then invested in safe assets because you can't afford to lose as much as you age and you're more reliant on investment capital.

(To get a complimentary risk score, go to: https://capstone planning.com/book.)

TYPES OF INVESTORS
CONSERVATIVE INVESTOR

A conservative investor primarily focuses on preserving capital and generating steady income, which is why their portfolio is heavily weighted toward fixed-income investments, such as bonds. Typically, 85 percent of their investment portfolio is allocated to bonds, which offer regular interest payments and have lower risk compared to equities. The remaining 15 percent is invested in stocks or equities, providing some growth potential without significantly increasing overall risk.

- Risk tolerance: Low
- Objective: Capital preservation and steady income
- Growth potential: Limited due to minimal exposure to stocks
- Volatility: Low, with stable returns from bonds

By maintaining a high percentage of bonds, conservative investors can rest assured that their income will remain relatively stable. However, this approach also means limited growth opportunities, as the potential for significant appreciation in stock investments is constrained.

MODERATE INVESTOR

A moderate investor balances the need for growth with the desire for stability by incorporating a more significant portion of equities into their portfolio. Typically, a moderate investor might allocate around 60 percent to bonds and 40 percent to stocks.

- Risk tolerance: Moderate
- Objective: Balanced approach to income and growth
- Growth potential: Moderate, with a balanced mix of bonds and stocks
- Volatility: Moderate, with a mix of stable bonds and more volatile stocks

This approach allows for higher growth potential compared to a conservative portfolio while still maintaining a level of stability through substantial bond holdings. Moderate investors are willing to accept more risk in exchange for better returns over the long term.

AGGRESSIVE INVESTOR

An aggressive investor prioritizes growth over stability and is willing to accept higher levels of risk. This investor typically allocates a significant portion of their portfolio to stocks and equities, often around 80–90 percent, with only 10–20 percent in bonds.

- Risk tolerance: High
- Objective: Maximum capital appreciation
- Growth potential: High, with significant exposure to equities
- Volatility: High, with potential for substantial gains and losses

By focusing primarily on stocks, aggressive investors aim for higher returns, acknowledging the increased volatility and risk that comes with it. This strategy is suitable for those with a longer investment horizon and the ability to withstand market fluctuations.

SUMMARY OF INVESTMENT APPROACHES

Conservative Investor:

- 85 percent bonds, 15 percent stocks
- Focus on capital preservation and steady income
- Low risk, low growth potential

Moderate Investor:

- 60 percent bonds, 40 percent stocks
- Balanced approach to income and growth
- Moderate risk, moderate growth potential

Aggressive Investor:

- 80–90 percent stocks, 10–20 percent bonds
- Focus on maximum capital appreciation
- High risk, high growth potential

Each investment strategy aligns with different financial goals and risk tolerances, helping investors choose the approach that best suits their needs and investment horizon.

Regardless of where you land on this spectrum, it's important to not only consider how much to invest, but also where to allocate your funds. Simply taking a percentage of your portfolio and investing into one company's stocks is not a flexible plan that can hold up under various market fluctuations. We don't just want a risky or a safe portfolio—we want a *smart* portfolio.

A smart portfolio includes a variety of investments based on your risk tolerance and capacity that we previously determined. Certain investments are considered riskier when the potential return is very high but the risk of loss is also high. Investments are considered safer when both the return and the risk of losing a lot of money are lower.

SMART DIVERSIFICATION

When Dave came into our office, he was six months out from retirement and wanted to make sure he had crossed his t's and dotted his i's. We took a look at his investment portfolio, and I noticed that all of his stocks were with General Electric. This guy had worked for GE most of his life, clearly loved the company, and felt a strong sense of loyalty to them.

"I understand you love GE," I said, "but if that company ever experiences a significant decline, it would put an enormous strain on your retirement."

He wasn't convinced this would ever happen, but his belief and trust in the company wouldn't be enough to protect him from a downfall. I explained to Dave that diversifying his portfolio wasn't a betrayal to the company, and they weren't going to call him and ask him what happened if he decided to sell some of his stocks.

I explained to him that these things *do* happen, that even some of the most stable stocks take a turn at times. Take Boeing, for example, whose stocks plummeted after one of their planes crashed in 2019. Or BP, whose stocks dropped significantly after an oil spill. I showed Dave what his numbers would look like if GE took a similar unexpected dip, and he didn't like what he saw.

A few months later, GE's stocks *did* drop—catastrophically. If Greg had stayed where he was, he would have been stuck drastically reducing spending and praying that GE would jump back up quickly. Thankfully, Greg had taken my advice and diversified his portfolio. At this point, he had invested in both a number of different options (bonds, stocks, annuities, etc.), as well as a variety within each category.

This goal of diversification is to have investments that move differently but overall positive over time. None of these investment options move the same. Historically, if your stocks or equity portions are way down, bonds are usually safer and may be generating around 4 or 5 percent. This also ensures that you stay invested even when certain elements of your portfolio drop.

Let's talk about some different investment streams and options within each one.

STOCKS

Stocks typically pertain to equity or ownership. In other words, you purchase a portion of the company. There are two ways that you can get return from a stock: capital appreciation and dividends. Capital appreciation is more common with newer companies that are growth-oriented. With more established companies (like ExxonMobil or Johnson & Johnson), shareholders receive a steady dividend.

BONDS

Think about bonds as buying debt from a company. If a company wants to go out and raise capital for a project, research, development, or another need, they'll issue bonds at a certain rate. You can buy and hold that debt, playing the role of the bank, and receive a certain percentage of credit on that debt. These rates are based on current interest rates so it's important to understand that bonds work like a seesaw. If bond rates go higher, the value of former bonds decreases. Conversely, if bond rates decrease, previous bondholders can sell their higher bonds at a premium.

Bonds are driven by interest rates. For a long time, they were known as the safety net of a portfolio because interest rates were dropping (we're talking the 1980s). And they have less wiggle room—you're not going to get large gains or large losses from bonds. Now, with high interest rates, bond values aren't as safe as they used to be.

INTERNATIONAL

There are options to invest in international stocks and bonds that move differently depending on the country and the market. There are pros and cons to investing in developed nations versus emerging markets around the world.

COMMODITIES

Commodities are raw materials or primary agricultural products that can be bought and sold. They are typically standardized and interchangeable with other goods of the same type. Investing in commodities involves trading these goods in various forms, including physical assets, futures contracts, and commodity-based financial instruments.

Commodities are broadly categorized into several types:

- Energy
- Metals

- Agricultural products
- Livestock

REAL ESTATE

Many people purchase real estate to establish an income stream through rent. You can also invest through real estate investment trusts (REITs), where you invest in a company that is purchasing real estate and collect a dividend from the income that the company earns.

ANNUITIES

Annuities are typically issued by an insurance company; you make a large payment or a series of smaller payments that gain interest and are then converted into recurring payments that can last for life. There are several different types of annuities, including:

- **Single premium immediate annuity (or SPIA):** You give an insurance company a lump sum of money. If you live a very long life, this is a great deal. However, if you pass early, you basically lose everything that you contributed. Because of this setup, SPIAs have become the least popular annuity option.
- **Variable annuity:** A variable annuity has something called subaccounts, where the money you contribute is still invested inside the market. That means it has the ups and downs of the market, along with some other features that guarantee income payments or death benefits. But this is also a costly way to own this type of asset, due to administrative and subaccount fees. I think of this option as a

Swiss Army knife—it does a lot, but doesn't do anything specifically well.

- **Index-based annuity:** These annuities are tied to the market, but are not actually in the market. This is the type of annuity we recommend because if the market goes down, you don't participate in the downside so your principal is always protected.
- **Multi-year guaranteed annuity (or MYGA):** These typically come in increments of two to ten years. These are similar to CDs in that they pay a fixed interest rate for a fixed period.

VOLATILITY BUFFER

An investment volatility buffer is a financial strategy or asset allocation designed to protect a portfolio against significant fluctuations in value due to market volatility. It aims to stabilize returns and minimize the impact of sudden market downturns on an investor's overall portfolio. Here's a more detailed description:

DESCRIPTION OF AN INVESTMENT VOLATILITY BUFFER

An investment volatility buffer is a safety net within an investment portfolio that helps mitigate the effects of market volatility. This buffer typically consists of low-risk, stable assets that are less susceptible to market fluctuations, thereby providing a cushion against losses during periods of high volatility. By incorporating a volatility buffer, investors can achieve more consistent returns and reduce the potential for substantial losses.

KEY COMPONENTS TO AN INVESTMENT VOLATILITY BUFFER

Cash and Cash Equivalents:

- Assets such as savings accounts, money market funds, and Treasury bills that offer liquidity and stability.

High-Quality Bonds:

- Government bonds or investment-grade corporate bonds that provide steady income and lower volatility compared to stocks.

Defensive Stocks:

- Stocks in sectors like utilities, consumer staples, and healthcare that tend to be less affected by economic downturns.

Alternative Investments:

- Assets like gold, real estate, or commodities that may not correlate directly with stock market performance and can provide diversification benefits.

BENEFITS OF AN INVESTMENT VOLATILITY BUFFER

Reduced Portfolio Risk:

- By including low-risk assets, the overall risk of the portfolio is reduced, making it less susceptible to severe market downturns.

Smoother Returns:

- The buffer helps smooth out the returns over time, leading to a more stable and predictable investment performance.

Emotional Comfort:

- Knowing there is a protective layer in place can help investors remain calm during volatile markets, reducing the likelihood of panic selling and poor investment decisions.

Liquidity:

- Having a portion of the portfolio in liquid assets ensures that investors have access to funds when needed, without having to sell volatile assets at a loss.

IMPLEMENTATION

To implement an investment volatility buffer, investors should: Assess Risk Tolerance:

- Determine how much risk they are willing to accept, and allocate a proportionate amount of their portfolio to low-risk, stable assets.

Diversify:

- Spread investments across various asset classes to ensure that the portfolio is not overly exposed to any single type of risk.

Regularly Rebalance:

- Periodically review and adjust the portfolio to maintain the desired level of risk and ensure the buffer remains effective.

Example

Imagine an investor with a $100,000 portfolio wants to protect against market volatility. They might allocate 60 percent ($60,000) to stocks and 40 percent ($40,000) to a volatility buffer consisting of high-quality bonds and cash equivalents. During a market downturn, the bonds and cash would provide stability and reduce the overall impact on the portfolio's value.

In summary, an investment volatility buffer is a strategic allocation of low-risk assets within a portfolio designed to cushion against market volatility, providing more consistent returns and reducing overall risk.

Now that we have a better understanding of investment options, let's talk taxes.

CHAPTER 5

≡

TAX PLANNING

We had a crowd of soon-to-be retirees gathered on a Tuesday evening at the local community center for one of our riveting tax-planning workshops.

"Let's start this party off right," I said. "With a quick poll, of course. How many of you think taxes will be lower in the future?"

One gentleman in the back emphatically raised his hand. All heads turned to peer at this optimistic outcast while he grinned sheepishly.

"Okay," I said. "How many people think taxes will be *higher* in the future?"

Everyone else raised their hands.

Despite the back-row gentleman's greatest hopes, there's no real evidence that taxes are going to go down...well, ever. We only have to look at simple numbers to wrap our heads around why.

If your household budget is $45,000 and you are projecting

that you'll spend $62,000 a year, is this a problem? Well, yes. Obviously. But if you catch this ahead of time, you can make some changes to fill this gap—reduce spending, get a part-time job, downgrade your home, or sell an asset or two.

Now let's look at this on a grander scale: the United State's 2023 federal budget was $4.5 trillion. However, federal spending was $6.2 trillion. Same problem. Much bigger household.

Much like a personal budget, we can solve this deficiency by reducing spending or identifying additional income. Let me ask you this: Do you think the government is going to reduce spending anytime soon? Right. So the only real option is increasing income. In other words, raising taxes.

Now, before I lose you on a federal tax rate tangent, let me assure you that, tax-wise, we're in a pretty decent spot compared to some years of old. For example, during World War II (1944–1945), the highest federal marginal tax rate was 94 percent. Yes, you read that correctly—94 percent—meaning, if you were in the top tax bracket, you would get to keep *six cents* for every dollar you earned.

Fun fact: this is the reason why Ronald Reagan would only star in one or two movies a year. If he claimed any more income, he'd be bumped up to the top tax bracket ($200,000 or more, at the time) and be liable for 94 percent of his earnings. If you went to work and took home six cents on the dollar, how motivated would you be to go out and hustle?

Compare that 94 percent to our current top tax rate of 37 percent (as of 2024), and perhaps this can help quiet some rants. In fact, it appears that taxes are on sale right now!

While taxes might be relatively low now, these current laws will expire in 2025. Knowing what we know about historical tax rates and our continued propensity for national debt, we can intelligently assume that taxes will likely increase in the future.

If Congress does nothing (and they're pretty good at doing nothing), taxes *will be higher* for the vast majority of people in 2025. So the question becomes, how do we protect against these potential upswings? How do we ensure we're not giving more to Uncle Sam than we need to?

In this chapter, we'll identify a few strategies to reduce taxable assets, diversify tax holdings, and avoid unnecessary penalties. All for the sake of maximizing the money you have in order to make your retirement life the best it can possibly be.

THE THREE TAX BUCKETS

Same workshop, same poll: I asked the gang, "What do you think will be your largest expense in retirement?"

One woman said, "Travel?"

Another, "Our mortgage?"

The guy in the back, "New golf clubs?"

I nodded along with their answers. I had heard them all before.

"Anyone know how much your annual tax bill will be in retirement?" I was fairly certain no one knew the answer to this question, and I consider it part of my job to enlighten people.

Here's the truth: most of our clients have an annual tax bill of around $15,000. You might never see this grand total written down anywhere because a lot of your taxes—Social Security, pensions, and investments—are withheld prior to hitting a bank account. But that doesn't mean this money doesn't exist. In fact, if you break it down to a monthly expense, we're talking over $1,000 per month. This is far more than most spend on travel or even a mortgage at this stage in the game.

I enlighten you not to discourage you, but to point out the vastness of that sum and to inspire you to think about how to diversify your tax holdings so that you can reduce this number as much as possible. Most of our clients come in with around 95 percent of their retirement savings in tax-deferred accounts (and perhaps a bit of cash in the bank).

However, there are *three* tax buckets: tax-deferred, after-tax, and tax-free. In the same way we want to diversify our investment portfolio, we also want to diversify our tax holdings. And ideally, we want more money in the tax-free category so that we ultimately owe less to the government. That's where our work today begins.

First, let's take a look at the three buckets:

TAX-DEFERRED

Definition: Tax-deferred investments allow you to postpone paying taxes on the income and gains until you withdraw the money. This means the investments can grow without the drag of annual taxes, potentially leading to larger compounded growth.

Examples

Traditional IRA:

- Contributions to a traditional IRA may be tax-deductible, and investments grow tax-deferred. Taxes are paid when withdrawals are made in retirement.
- Example: If you contribute $5,000 to a traditional IRA, that amount is not taxed in the year you contribute. The account grows tax-deferred, and when you retire and withdraw funds, the amount withdrawn is taxed as ordinary income.

401(k) Plan:

- Contributions to a 401(k) plan are made with pretax dollars, reducing taxable income for the year. The investments grow tax-deferred, and taxes are paid upon withdrawal.
- Example: If you contribute $10,000 to a 401(k), that $10,000 is not included in your taxable income for that year. The investments grow tax-deferred until you withdraw the funds in retirement, at which point the withdrawals are taxed as ordinary income.

AFTER-TAX

Definition: After-tax investments are made with money that has already been taxed. The investment income (such as interest, dividends, and capital gains) is subject to taxes in the year it is earned.

Examples

Roth IRA:

- Contributions to a Roth IRA are made with after-tax dollars. The investments grow tax-free, and qualified withdrawals in retirement are also tax-free.
- Example: If you contribute $5,000 to a Roth IRA, you pay taxes on that $5,000 in the year of contribution. The investments grow tax-free, and when you withdraw the money in retirement, the withdrawals are tax-free.

Brokerage Account:

- Investments made through a standard brokerage account are made with after-tax dollars. You pay taxes on dividends, interest, and capital gains in the year they are earned or realized.
- Example: If you invest $10,000 in stocks through a brokerage account, you have already paid taxes on that $10,000. Any dividends or capital gains from selling stocks are taxed in the year they are received.

TAX-FREE

Definition: Tax-free investments are those where the earnings or withdrawals are not subject to federal income tax. Some may also be free from state and local taxes.

Examples

Municipal Bonds:

- Interest earned on municipal bonds is generally tax-free at the federal level and may also be exempt from state and local taxes if you reside in the issuing state.
- Example: If you purchase a municipal bond for $10,000 with a 3 percent interest rate, you earn $300 in interest annually. This interest is typically exempt from federal income tax, and if you live in the state that issued the bond, it may also be exempt from state and local taxes.

Health Savings Account (HSA):

- Contributions to an HSA are made with pretax dollars, the investments grow tax-free, and withdrawals for qualified medical expenses are also tax-free.

- Example: If you contribute $3,500 to an HSA, you get a tax deduction for that amount. The investments grow tax-free, and when you withdraw funds to pay for medical expenses, those withdrawals are tax-free.

SUMMARY

- Tax-Deferred: Taxes are postponed until withdrawals are made (e.g., traditional IRA, 401(k)).
- After-Tax: Investments are made with already-taxed money, and income is taxed when earned (e.g., Roth IRA, brokerage account).
- Tax-Free: Earnings or withdrawals are not subject to federal taxes (e.g., municipal bonds, HSA).

Our mission, then, becomes moving money from the tax-deferred category to the tax-free category. Sound complicated? I assure you, it's not, but I also encourage enlisting the help of a CPA or financial advisor as you start making these moves. Before you decide on anything, let's take a closer look at Roth IRAs as they are the golden ticket to diversifying your tax holdings and reducing your overall contributions to Uncle Sam's accounts.

ROTH IRAS

Imagine you're planting a crop, starting with a handful of seeds. In traditional tax-deferred vehicles, the seeds aren't taxed but the harvest is 100 percent taxable at regular income rates. So while you may not pay taxes up front, you pay a ton on the withdrawal. Roth IRAs use after-tax dollars to generate tax-free growth. In other words, the seed *is* taxed, but the great big harvest is 100 percent *tax free*. Would you rather pay tax on the seed or the harvest?

Most people didn't realize that they had a partner—a.k.a., Uncle Sam—when they were investing for retirement. Part of every dollar that you take from a tax-deferred vehicle goes to this greedy guy. If you have $1 million in a tax-deferred holding, how much money do you really have? It depends on your tax bracket, but definitely less than $1 million, when it's all said and done.

If you have $1 million in a Roth IRA, how much money do you really have? Simple: $1 million (because Roth IRAs are tax-free when you want to distribute the funds).

You might be wondering if you have enough time to invest in a Roth account, but rest assured that if you're on the cusp of retirement, you likely have another twenty to thirty years of life yet to live. Your runway is plenty long to make some moves that will give you a lot of flexibility, buffers, and assurance later on. Now let's consider a few ways you can take tax-deferred dollars and put them into a tax-free account.

ROTH CONVERSIONS

The more you can turn taxable money into tax-free dollars, the more you can control your tax bracket in retirement. One popular strategy is called incremental Roth conversions, which is an efficient twofold process. First, you pay the tax on the tax-deferred money. Then you convert it into a Roth IRA, or tax-free dollars. (The only rule that can make the gains taxable is if you do not meet the five-year rule, which states that the conversion must have occurred five years prior to you taking out the gains.)

For example: Jim wants to convert $100,000 of his traditional IRA into Roth dollars over the next five years. Instead of converting the full $100,000 in one pass, Jim will do this incrementally, in $20,000 allotments, to allow for a lower annual taxation fee. In year one, Jim's account gains 20 percent, or $4,000. That means he can take out the original $20,000 with no tax penalty, but he has to wait five more years on the additional $4,000 (to not face a penalty). If he finds himself in a situation where he needs to pull all of the money out ahead of the five-year timeline, he would simply pull out the funds and pay regular income tax rates on the gains (as if it were a tax-deferred account).

BRACKET BUMPING EXPLAINED

Bracket bumping is a tax strategy where you convert a portion of your tax-deferred retirement savings, like a traditional IRA, into a Roth IRA. The key is to convert just enough so that you stay within your current tax bracket, thereby avoiding a higher tax rate.

Example: Karen's Roth Conversion

Scenario:

- Karen earns $65,000 per year.
- She consults her tax professional and financial advisor to implement a bracket bumping strategy.
- They decide to convert some of her tax-deferred money to a Roth IRA without pushing her into a higher tax bracket.

Using 2024 tax brackets for single filers:

- The 22 percent tax bracket for single filers ranges from $47,151 to $100,525.
- Karen's taxable income is $65,000.
- To stay within the 22 percent tax bracket, Karen can convert up to $35,525 of her tax-deferred money to a Roth IRA ($100,525 – $65,000 = $35,525).

Calculation:

- Maximum allowable conversion without moving to the next bracket:
  - $100,525 (upper limit of the 22 percent bracket) – $65,000 (Karen's income) = $35,525.

Result:

- Karen converts $35,525 from her traditional IRA to a Roth IRA.
- This conversion is taxed at her current 22 percent tax rate.
- By doing this, Karen ensures that the converted amount grows tax-free in the Roth IRA and avoids being pushed into the 24 percent tax bracket.

Benefits of Bracket Bumping

Tax Efficiency:

- Karen maximizes the use of her current tax bracket, converting as much as possible without incurring a higher tax rate.

Future Tax-Free Growth:

- The converted amount in the Roth IRA will grow tax-free, and qualified withdrawals in retirement will not be taxed.

Strategic Planning:

- By spreading out conversions over several years, Karen can manage her tax liability each year, potentially reducing her overall lifetime tax burden.

Summary

Bracket bumping allows Karen to convert $35,525 from a traditional IRA to a Roth IRA without moving into a higher tax bracket. This strategic move helps her manage her taxes efficiently and ensures her investments grow tax-free in the future.

MARKET TIMING ROTH CONVERSION STRATEGY

Explanation: Market timing Roth conversion is a strategy where you convert a portion of your traditional IRA to a Roth IRA during a market downturn. The idea is to take advantage of lower asset values, reducing the amount of tax paid on the conversion. Once the market recovers, the growth in the Roth IRA is tax-free.

Example: Bill's Roth Conversion

Scenario:

- Bill has $300,000 in his traditional IRA.
- He wants to convert $20,000 to a Roth IRA in 2020.

Market Timing:

- In 2020, the market dipped significantly in February and March due to the COVID-19 economic shutdown.
- Bill decided to convert $20,000 during this market dip.

Result:

- After the conversion, the market recovered over the next several months.
- Bill's traditional IRA grew back to $312,000.
- His Roth IRA, which was funded with the $20,000 conversion, grew to $26,000.

Benefit:

- The $6,000 growth in the Roth IRA is entirely tax-free.
- This strategy can be visualized like a slinky: when the market contracts (slinky contracts), you convert the funds. When the market expands (slinky expands), all gains in the Roth account are tax-free.

Benefits of Market Timing Roth Conversion

Tax Efficiency:

- By converting during a market dip, you pay taxes on a lower account value, potentially reducing your tax liability.

Tax-Free Growth:

- Any subsequent growth in the Roth IRA is tax-free, providing a significant benefit if the market recovers strongly.

Strategic Conversion:

- This strategy allows for a more strategic approach to Roth conversions, optimizing the timing to maximize tax benefits.

Key Considerations

Market Timing Risks:

- Accurately timing the market is challenging and can be risky. Market conditions are unpredictable, and conversions based solely on market timing can lead to suboptimal results if mistimed.

Tax Implications:

- Even though the converted amount may be lower during a market dip, it's essential to consider the overall tax impact and your current tax bracket.

Financial Planning:

- Consult with a financial advisor to determine the appropriate amount to convert and the optimal timing, considering your overall financial plan and retirement goals.

Summary

Market timing Roth conversion is a strategic approach to converting traditional IRA funds to a Roth IRA during market downturns. By taking advantage of lower asset values, investors can reduce their tax liability on the conversion amount. Subsequent market recoveries lead to tax-free growth within the Roth IRA, enhancing the overall benefit of the conversion.

Example Recap

- Bill converted $20,000 during a market dip when his traditional IRA was valued at $300,000.
- Post-recovery, his traditional IRA is worth $312,000, and his Roth IRA has grown to $26,000.
- The $6,000 growth in the Roth IRA is tax-free, showcasing the advantage of this strategy.

Using these methods, we can offset the risk of higher taxes in the future. It's important to say again that we highly recommend implementing these strategies with the help of a tax and financial professional. There are certain nuances and considerations that can have a long-term impact on Medicare and other aspects of your financial portfolio. Which brings us to another important consideration—avoiding penalties.

AVOID UNNECESSARY PENALTIES

As we discussed regarding Social Security, most people are unaware of the hidden requirements and penalties in certain government-issued policies. These fines add up, sometimes to a substantial amount of money. Sometimes, they can even change the trajectory of a surviving spouse's financial future.

We'll discuss several more common penalties and how to steer clear of these blunders.

REQUIRED MINIMUM DISTRIBUTION

Withdrawing money from your retirement accounts before age fifty-nine and a half usually results in a 10 percent IRS penalty. However, if you don't start taking required minimum distributions (RMDs) by age seventy-three (or seventy-five, if you were born on or after 1960), you could face a 25 percent tax penalty. For example, if you have $500,000 in your traditional IRA and forget to withdraw $20,000 when required, the IRS will penalize you an additional $5,000.

This penalty is due to RMD rules, which mandate that you start withdrawing a certain percentage, typically starting around 4 percent. Missing these withdrawals can push you into higher tax brackets and increase your exposure to investment taxes and/or income-related monthly adjustment amount charges.

How to avoid this: Ideally, you should set up your IRA withdrawal on autopilot, to ensure that it's systematic and preplanned so that even if you are completely incapacitated, you won't face this 25 percent tax hit. (I personally would not rely on the heart of the IRS to waive these penalties, regardless of your unfortunate circumstances.)

Another strategy to consider, particularly if you already donate a substantial amount of money, is a qualified charitable donation (or QCD). You can actually reduce the taxes on your RMD by sending funds directly to a registered church or charity (and, no, unfortunately your kids are not considered a charity).

Qualified Charitable Donations Explained

A qualified charitable donation (QCD) allows individuals who are seventy and a half years or older to donate up to $100,000 per year directly from their individual retirement account (IRA) to a qualified charity without having to pay income taxes on the distribution. This can be a beneficial strategy for meeting required minimum distributions (RMDs) and reducing taxable income.

Key Points of Qualified Charitable Donations

Eligibility:

- Individuals must be at least seventy and a half years old at the time of the donation.
- The donation must be made from a traditional IRA or an inherited IRA. Roth IRAs can also be used, but distributions are usually tax-free regardless.

Annual Limit:

- The maximum amount that can be donated as a QCD is $105,000 per year (as of 2024), per individual. For married couples, each spouse can donate up to $105,000 from their own IRAs.

Tax Benefits:

- QCDs can satisfy RMD requirements for the year.
- The donated amount is excluded from taxable income, which can be particularly advantageous as it may lower the donor's adjusted gross income (AGI) and potentially reduce the impact of other taxes and phaseouts.

Qualified Charities:

- Donations must be made to a 501(c)(3) organization that is eligible to receive tax-deductible charitable contributions. Donor-advised funds and private foundations do not qualify.

Direct Transfer:

- The donation must be made directly from the IRA custodian to the charity. If the IRA owner receives the funds first and then donates them, the distribution will be taxed as income.

Example Scenario

Imagine John, who is seventy-two years old, has an IRA and is required to take an RMD of $25,000 for the year. He prefers not to increase his taxable income, so he decides to make a QCD.

- John donates $25,000 directly from his IRA to his favorite qualified charity.
- This donation satisfies his RMD requirement for the year.
- The $25,000 is excluded from his taxable income, which helps him avoid higher taxes and potentially reduces the impact on his Social Security benefits and Medicare premiums.

Advantages of QCDs

Tax Savings:

- By excluding the donation from taxable income, QCDs can help lower the donor's tax liability.

- Reducing AGI can help mitigate the impact on income-sensitive items like Social Security benefits and Medicare premiums.

Charitable Impact:

- Donors can support their favorite charities with significant contributions.
- QCDs offer a tax-efficient way to fulfill philanthropic goals.

RMD Satisfaction:

- QCDs count toward satisfying RMDs, allowing retirees to meet this requirement without increasing their taxable income.

Key Considerations

- Documentation: Ensure proper documentation and confirmation from the charity to substantiate the QCD.
- Deadline: The QCD must be completed by December 31 of the tax year to count toward that year's RMD.
- IRA Types: Ensure the donation is from an eligible IRA account.

Summary

Qualified charitable donations offer a tax-efficient way for individuals aged seventy and a half and older to donate to charities directly from their IRAs, reduce their taxable income, and satisfy their RMDs. By understanding the rules and benefits, retirees can make significant charitable contributions while optimizing their tax situation.

BENEFICIARIES OF TAX-DEFERRED ACCOUNTS

Right now, if your spouse is listed as your 100 percent primary beneficiary on a tax-deferred account (IRA, 401(k), 403(b)), it becomes their account in the case of your passing. No taxes are immediately owed on these funds. However, if a non-spouse (give or take a couple of exemptions) is listed as beneficiary, this person has ten years to spend the money down (a change via the SECURE Act of 2020).

UNDERSTANDING SOCIAL SECURITY TAXATION AND PROVISIONAL INCOME

Social Security Taxation: Social Security benefits are not inherently taxable. However, they may be taxed based on your provisional income, ranging from 0 percent to 85 percent.

Provisional Income: This includes your adjusted gross income (AGI), nontaxable interest, and half of your Social Security benefits. Importantly, Roth IRA withdrawals are not included in this calculation, making them advantageous for tax purposes.

Real-Life Scenario: John and Sally (2024 Tax Laws)

Before John's death:

- John and Sally, married and filing jointly, are both over sixty-five.
- They need $60,000 per year for living expenses.
- John's Social Security: $20,000
- Sally's Social Security: $10,000
- IRA Distributions: $30,000

- Total Provisional Income: $45,000 (half of their combined Social Security benefits + IRA distributions)
- Based on these numbers, they owe $455 in taxes.

After John's death:

- Sally still needs $60,000 per year for living expenses.
- She receives John's higher Social Security benefit: $20,000.
- She pulls $40,000 from the IRA.
- Now filing as a single person, her taxes increase significantly.
- Her provisional income is $50,000 (half of her Social Security benefit + IRA distributions).
- Her federal taxes rose from $455 to over $4,622, a *915 percent increase*, due to higher taxable income and the change in filing status.

How to Mitigate This Tax Impact

Using Roth IRA: If Sally could withdraw the extra $10,000 from a Roth IRA, her taxes would be much lower. Roth IRA withdrawals do not count toward provisional income, reducing taxable income.

Tax Scenario with Roth IRA:

- Social Security: $20,000
- IRA Distributions: $30,000
- Additional $10,000 from Roth IRA
- Provisional Income: $40,000 (half of her Social Security + IRA distributions, excluding Roth withdrawals)
- Her federal taxes would be $2,534, significantly lower than $4,622.

Summary

Understanding how Social Security benefits are taxed based on provisional income and leveraging Roth IRAs can significantly reduce your tax burden in retirement. By planning ahead and using Roth conversions or contributions, you can avoid unexpected tax increases, especially after the loss of a spouse.

SIMPLIFIED POINTS

- Social Security Taxation: Based on provisional income, 0 percent to 85 percent taxable.
- Provisional Income: Includes AGI, nontaxable interest, half of Social Security benefits; excludes Roth IRA withdrawals.
- Example Scenario: John and Sally's taxes increase from $455 to $4,622 after John's death due to changes in provisional income and filing status.
- Mitigation Strategy: Use Roth IRA withdrawals to reduce taxable income, resulting in lower taxes.
- By strategically planning and understanding these tax implications, retirees can optimize their income and minimize taxes.

Hopefully you now have a better understanding of how different retirement savings accounts are taxed so that you can make educated decisions. All of this—whether moving money into tax-free accounts or avoiding penalties—works toward the broader goal of making sure you don't run out of money and living the best retirement life possible.

Now that we've established your income streams and investment options and identified ways to reduce your contributions to Uncle Sam, we want to make sure this plan will work, no matter what state of health you find yourself in. In the next chapter, we'll make sure you're covered in sickness and in health.

CHAPTER 6

HEALTHCARE PLANNING

Tom and Phyllis retired with about $1 million in assets. As I always do, I encouraged them to consider protecting this money with a long-term care policy, just in case anyone got sick. They decided not to and signed our agreement stating that they were refusing long-term care. A few years later, Tom was diagnosed with Alzheimer's disease.

He's now been in a memory care facility for over five years, where they pay $7,500 a month and an additional $2,600 for twenty-four-hour care—over $10,000 a month and $120,000 per year. Note, this is in addition to all their regular living expenses. Now multiply that by several years, and their $1 million in assets is disappearing rapidly. The reality is that Tom and Phyllis will likely deplete their entire portfolio before he passes away. Not only will Phyllis be left without Tom's pension and her Social Security, but she also won't have an investment portfolio stream of income either.

"How much longer can I afford this?" Phyllis recently asked me.

This is exactly the scenario we want to avoid, and also the reason we stress the importance of having a healthcare plan. The interesting thing about long-term care is that it's really designed for the more affluent because they have more to protect. If you have fewer assets, at the end of the day, you can always choose to spend those assets down and go on Medicaid. While Medicaid isn't the most attractive option, going on vacations may sound more appealing than paying for a long-term care policy. So some people will plan to spend down their assets and eventually go on Medicaid. It's at least a plan, which is more than I can say for many retirees, but not a great one. And there are other options.

PROTECTING LOVED ONES

To be honest, this isn't the most exciting part of the planning process. No one wants to think of themselves getting sick or dying. They'd rather put their head in the sand and avoid the thought altogether. Putting a plan in place can make that future possibility a little too real.

I will say that our clients that have had to care for a sick or dying parent are far more receptive to this conversation. In fact, they typically jump on putting a plan into place, having lived the hard reality of either tending to the daily care of or participating in paying for long-term care for an older adult. Often, when finances haven't been designated to cover long-term healthcare expenses, this responsibility falls onto loved ones—a spouse, children, or grandchildren.

Take Jeff, for example. He lost his wife many years ago to pancreatic cancer, and has been living alone since then, many states away from his three children. His health is declining, and as it has become more difficult for him to drive, walk, and keep up with his medications, his children are worried. Furthermore, his memory is starting to decline, and his kids don't want him living alone anymore. Unfortunately, Jeff doesn't have a long-term healthcare policy. And while Medicare may cover some in-home expenses, he's on the verge of needing around-the-clock care.

His three kids are having stressful conversations about what to do and what they can afford. Paying out-of-pocket for a nursing home doesn't seem feasible. None of them want to take on the responsibility of caring for an aging adult full-time, who is in the early stages of dementia—they all have young children of their own and demanding careers. At the end of the day, they feel stuck. If Jeff had an LTC insurance policy in place, this scenario would look a lot different for all parties involved.

The truth is, long-term care usually entails much more than one of your children popping by your home to feed you a sandwich and a bowl of soup. You may need in-home care, a nursing home, or a memory care facility, all of which cost quite a bit of money. Not to mention the astronomical inflation rate related to healthcare right now. The bottom line is: if you don't want to be a burden on your family and do want to ensure you get quality care (which you absolutely deserve), then take the time to put a viable plan into place.

Healthcare planning is a vital piece of the puzzle. I cannot stress that enough. It accounts for 20 percent of your plan's effectiveness. If it's not part of your plan, it's like venturing out into the open seas with a hole in your boat. You're going to take in water at some point in time. And, like Tom and Phyllis, you might watch your hard-earned money and investments dwindle away very quickly. What a stressful and disappointing end to the story, all because they were unwilling to allocate funds for long-term care. Thankfully, Tom and Phyllis have been able to pay for his care thus far, but many others aren't so lucky.

GATHERING DATA

The national annual median cost for a private room in a nursing home is $106,000 per year (as of 2024). Now this number can vary based on your location and type of care facility. But, without a doubt, this expense can absolutely devastate a family over time. You may be thinking (as many do), *I don't need long-term care. I'm going to die peacefully in my sleep at age seventy-eight.* However, studies show that 70 percent of sixty-five-year-olds today will need some type of long-term care down the road. That means, more likely than not, you need to consider this as part of your retirement plan.

If you don't have money set aside and you find yourself in need of more attentive care, are you going to pay for a spot at a skilled nursing facility? Probably not. Instead, you're far more likely to suffer through these difficult years for as long as you can bear it so that you don't have to put a strain on your finances or your family.

However, with a plan in place, you can be more selective about what type of facility you choose, and you'll also be far more likely to use it. So, while not the most engaging or fun conversation, I want you to take the time to think about these things. If you were to need long-term healthcare:

- Where would you want to go?
- How much does a facility like this cost?
- How much does home healthcare in your area cost, on average?

- How will you pay for it?

We recommend that you actually go visit some of the nearby long-term care facilities to get an idea of what they look like and how much they cost. The more data that you can gather regarding cost, the better prepared you can be in setting money aside in this healthcare bucket. Seeing these places up close and personal can also help paint a picture of what life there would look like. Many people have misinformed notions about nursing homes—that they are depressing, demeaning, or lonely—and touring these places can help you find an appealing option if you ever find yourself in need. Being the one to decide on this also helps the transition so that your loved ones aren't forced to make decisions about your long-term care needs without your input.

Some of our clients even pay money up front to get on a list at prepaid nursing homes. They're expensive, but they are phenomenal facilities, and if these individuals don't use their spot, the facility may refund their beneficiaries.

Regardless of the path you choose, there are several ways you can financially plan for long-term care. While Medicare may offer limited coverage for some beneficiaries (like outpatient therapy or some home health options), it won't cover assisted living costs. We'll talk about several long-term healthcare investment options, but first, let's talk about Medicare and how it plays a part in your healthcare needs throughout retirement.

MEDICARE OVERVIEW

Medicare is the federal health insurance program primarily for individuals aged sixty-five and older, but it also covers some younger people with disabilities. It is divided into four parts, each covering different aspects of healthcare.

MEDICARE PART A: HOSPITAL INSURANCE

- Coverage: Inpatient hospital stays, care in a skilled nursing facility, hospice care, and some home healthcare.
- Costs: Generally free for most people who have paid Medicare taxes for at least ten years. Otherwise, a premium may apply. There are also deductibles and coinsurance for services.

MEDICARE PART B: MEDICAL INSURANCE

- Coverage: Doctors' services, outpatient care, medical supplies, and preventive services.
- Costs: Part B has a monthly premium, which can vary based on income. There is also an annual deductible and typically 20 percent coinsurance for services after the deductible is met.

MEDICARE PART C: MEDICARE ADVANTAGE

- Coverage: Includes all benefits and services under Parts A and B. Most plans also include Part D (prescription drug coverage) and may offer extra coverage, such as vision, hearing, and dental.
- Structure: Offered by Medicare-approved private insurance companies. Costs and coverage details vary by plan.
- Benefits: Can provide additional services beyond Original Medicare, often with lower out-of-pocket costs.

MEDICARE PART D: PRESCRIPTION DRUG COVERAGE

- Coverage: Helps cover the cost of prescription drugs, including many recommended shots or vaccines.
- Costs: Part D plans are offered by Medicare-approved private insurers and have varying premiums, deductibles, and co-payments.
- Structure: Each plan has a formulary, which is a list of covered drugs. Plans can vary widely in terms of cost and specific drug coverage.

KEY POINTS

- Part A: Hospital stays and inpatient care; usually free.
- Part B: Outpatient care and doctor visits; monthly premium and co-pays.
- Part C: Combines A and B, often with additional benefits; offered by private insurers.
- Part D: Prescription drug coverage; offered by private insurers with varying costs.

MEDIGAP (MEDICARE SUPPLEMENTS)

Medigap policies are additional insurance you can buy to cover the healthcare costs that Medicare doesn't pay, such as co-payments, coinsurance, and deductibles. They help reduce your out-of-pocket expenses, making healthcare more affordable.

Understanding these parts can help you make informed decisions about your Medicare coverage to ensure you get the healthcare you need while managing your costs effectively. For detailed and personalized advice, it's always good to consult with a Medicare specialist or your healthcare provider.

In the past, you could switch Medicare plans. People would save money by signing up for more basic plans at the beginning of retirement and then, when they'd get sick, they would switch over to the better plans. But Medicare got wise to this. Now you have to qualify for a medigap policy (supplement) for anything beyond your initial enrollment. You have an initial enrollment at sixty-five (or whenever you retire) where there are no health qualifications. That's why we highly recommend giving this some serious thought and also taking the supplement from the get-go. If you ever give it up and shift to an Advantage Plan, you have to qualify for other plans, and good luck trying to qualify at age seventy-five for anything aside from a discount at the movie theater!

LONG-TERM HEALTHCARE POLICIES

In addition to Medicare, it's wise to have a long-term care policy that covers home healthcare and nursing home facilities. There are three main types of long-term care insurance: self-insured, traditional long-term care insurance, and asset-based long-term care insurance. We often recommend asset-based long-term care insurance for its flexibility and benefits.

SELF-INSURED

One way to cover long-term care costs is by using your own assets. For example, one client, a single woman, planned to sell her second home in Colorado, valued at over $1 million, if she needed long-term care. This is a self-insured option, where you rely on personal assets to cover future healthcare costs.

TRADITIONAL LONG-TERM CARE INSURANCE

With traditional long-term care insurance, you pay regular premiums in exchange for a fixed daily benefit, such as $200 per day for in-home care or nursing-home care. This option tends to be more affordable if purchased in your forties or early fifties but can become prohibitively expensive if bought later in life.

A downside is that premiums can increase annually, sometimes up to 10 percent, making it unaffordable over time. Additionally, if the policy is never used, you lose all the money paid in premiums.

Example: Liz bought a traditional long-term care policy at age forty-five with affordable premiums. By the time she turned eighty-five, her premiums had increased significantly, and she struggled to afford them on a fixed income.

ASSET-BASED LONG-TERM CARE INSURANCE

We often recommend asset-based long-term care insurance, which combines life insurance with a long-term care rider. You can pay premiums monthly or in a lump sum.

Example: If you have $250,000 in cash, it can be converted into $750,000 worth in long-term care benefits. These premiums do not increase, reducing the risk of future unaffordable costs. If long-term care isn't needed, the policy provides a tax-free death benefit to your beneficiaries.

Bob and Judy's Story

Bob and Judy, both sixty, buy an asset-based policy with a single premium of $158,682, which provides a lifetime benefit of $6,000 per person, per month for long-term care. If they never need it, their children will receive a $200,000 tax-free death benefit.

A few years later, Judy breaks her hip. Her policy covers her in-home care because she cannot perform two of the six activities of daily living (ADLs). If they use the entire $200,000, they will still have lifetime coverage.

Conclusion

Asset-based long-term care insurance can offer comprehensive coverage and ensures that even if you exceed your original policy, your long-term care needs are met. If you don't use it, the money goes to your beneficiaries, making it a versatile and secure choice.

GROW OLD IN PEACE

Rebecca had spent six years caring for her elderly mother, who didn't have a long-term healthcare plan in place. She even went through a nursing training program so that she could provide the care that her mother needed, without breaking the bank. It was a long, difficult journey for Rebecca, and it required her full attention. For the years she cared for her mother, she had to put many of her dreams on hold. She didn't take a promotion at work, stopped traveling, let her own health go, and experienced increased anxiety and depression. They were difficult years.

When we started to discuss Rebecca's retirement plan, and specifically a long-term healthcare plan, Rebecca agreed without hesitation that she wanted to invest a lump sum of money so that she could go to a facility, if needed, and above all else, protect her children from having to care for her in this way.

When we delivered her policy, Rebecca was in tears.

"Are you okay?" I asked her.

"Yes!" she replied. "I'm just so happy that I'm not going to be a burden to my daughter."

Now I can't say I've had this sort of response to an LTC policy often in my career, but it goes to show that to be on the caregiving side of things truly changes your perspective. Rebecca cared for her mother out of love and necessity, but that experience shaped her priorities. She didn't want to place that same burden on her daughter. Knowing that she had a plan in place that would prevent this outcome was a great relief to her, and this is exactly the kind of freedom and peace we want to bring to our clients.

If Tom or Jeff had taken the time and invested the money into an asset-based long-term healthcare policy, their stories would have played out much differently. Tom's wife, Phyllis, wouldn't be stressed about finances and wondering if and when she won't be able to pay for the care that Tom needs. And what then? Jeff's children wouldn't be wondering how their dad is going to live out the last of his days, what his quality of life will look like, and what they'll have to sacrifice in order to care for him well. How will this change the trajectory of their decisions and lives?

Long-term healthcare isn't just about you. It's about protecting the ones you love, setting them up to live out their days in peace, knowing that you are able to get the best quality care that you can. Now that you have a plan in place that covers income, investments, taxes, and healthcare, we move to the last piece of the puzzle—legacy planning—where we'll cover proper beneficiaries and designations to ensure that you are covered in life and in death.

CHAPTER 7

LEGACY PLANNING

When I was a child, my aunt married Peter, and they settled in Springfield, Illinois, with her three children from a previous marriage, who were then six, eight, and ten years old. She met Peter, the love of her life, while managing a restaurant.

Sadly, just a few years later, at the age of forty-five, Peter died unexpectedly from a heart embolism, passing away within hours. My aunt was left in shock and devastated by his sudden death.

A few weeks after Peter's death, my aunt met with their financial planner to review Peter's life insurance policy.

"Patty, it appears Peter's sister is listed as the beneficiary of this policy."

My aunt was speechless. How could Peter have named his sister as the beneficiary, overlooking her and the children? When she spoke with Peter's sister, explaining that he must have forgotten to update the beneficiary after their marriage, his sister replied, "No, I think he really wanted me to have this."

As a result, my aunt received nothing. She was left as a widow and a single mother, not only mourning the sudden loss of her husband but also faced with the challenge of supporting herself and three children on a single income.

This story obviously hits close to home, but it's also not an uncommon tale. We meet with clients on a regular basis who assume that their 401(k)s automatically transfer beneficiaries when they divorce or remarry. But when we take a look at the name on that line, it's an ex-wife or ex-husband. If this person were to die, the policy would go to the ex-wife or ex-husband— no questions asked. No contesting either because the courts will say, "We don't know the wishes of the deceased."

In the financial world, **legacy** refers to a financial inheritance that you pass on to loved ones or charities. In this last leg of *The Better Retirement Journey*™, you'll consider how you want to distribute your estate and ensure that everything is designated to pass correctly. The biggest to-do when it comes to legacy planning is making sure your beneficiaries are listed correctly. You may also want to consider setting up a trust and some other gifting strategies as you map out how your money will pass along after you're gone.

PASSING MONEY CORRECTLY

Who do you want your money to go to?

It's a simple question that holds a lot of weight, and we'll start here because the answer will determine the rest of your decisions. Do you have a spouse that will take over your accounts in the case of your death? Do you want to leave money for your children or grandchildren? For generations to come? To a charity or another nonprofit organization?

The vast majority of people want to leave their money to

their surviving spouse first and foremost, then to kids and grandkids, and then, sometimes, to a charitable organization. Once you establish how you want funds to pass along, you can double-check beneficiaries, perhaps set up a trust, and identify gifting strategies that will help you achieve your long-term legacy goals.

BENEFICIARIES

In our experience, people often set up a beneficiary and never revisit their decision. If the beneficiary is an ex-spouse (or a sibling like in my aunt's case), you will potentially leave your current spouse or children high and dry. That's why we recommend checking your beneficiary lines once a year to review how your assets and money will pass along and to make sure any changes are noted. We also typically draw a chart to illustrate primary beneficiaries and then contingent beneficiaries.

There are two types of beneficiary designations—per capita and per stirpes:

- **Per capita** means "by head." In this method, beneficiaries receive an inheritance based on specific designations. For example, you can divide your estate equally among your children or allocate specific amounts or assets to each child.
- **Per stirpes** means "by branch." In this method, the inheritance is distributed down the family line. Typically, the surviving spouse gets a large portion, and the remainder is passed down to children, grandchildren, and further descendants.

A bank account beneficiary is listed through a POD, or pay on death. It can be very difficult to access a person's bank account after they pass away. If you have a joint account, your spouse will have access, but designating a POD ensures that the next beneficiary has access in the event of both of your deaths. Your bank won't typically volunteer this service—you'll have to ask to see your title and fill in the spot for a POD, directly after the joint holder's name.

A TOD, or transfer on death, applies to accounts that aren't retirement accounts—money that's been saved and then invested in an after-tax or nonqualified account like a brokerage account. A TOD is a nonprobate way to transfer assets.

Finally, double-check all of the beneficiary lines on your retirement accounts—pensions, IRAs, 401(k)s, and 403(b)s. Make sure you have the correct beneficiary assigned to each one and revisit all of these designations once a year.

A reminder about maximizing tax benefits: If you want to designate a portion of your estate to a charity, I recommend considering appointing IRA assets (in other words, pretaxed assets) for this purpose. If you leave your IRA to a human being, they will have to pay taxes on it, but an IRA transfers to a charity tax-free.

TRUSTS

The only way to control money beyond the grave is through a trust. Trusts are helpful—and sometimes vital—in certain situations, particularly when a couple has a blended family with several kids from different marriages. If you're interested in setting up a trust, we encourage you to speak to an estate planning attorney to ensure that everything is established and can pass the way you want it to. Too often, people will create a trust and never make the trust the owner or the beneficiary. So the trust is empty. Unless the trust gets funded, there's really no point in having one.

For example, one of my clients spent a couple thousand dollars to set up a revocable trust. This was a smart move given their complex family situation which included multiple marriages and several children. They wanted to ensure their money would be distributed correctly. However, when we reviewed their accounts, we found they were all titled in their individual or joint names and also did not list the trust as the beneficiary of these accounts.

If you decide to set up a trust, I always recommend having one trustee rather than multiple trustees. From my experience, it can be a stressful and polarizing process when several siblings are cotrustees and are expected to agree on how an estate is distributed. It causes a lot of unnecessary angst. Pick one. Those who didn't get picked might have their feelings hurt for a little while, but it will be a much smoother process in the long run. You can designate one of your offspring or a close friend as trustee. Some people hire services (most banks have trustee services) with a fixed fee, but this can be expensive.

Also, make sure the person you choose is trustworthy. Technically they are held to a fiduciary duty, and they have to do what's in the best interest of the trust in how they distribute assets, but there aren't many checks and balances. Some family members might challenge it and then it will move into a court proceeding; this is a long and expensive process.

GIFTING STRATEGIES SIMPLIFIED

If you have assets that you won't use in your lifetime, consider these gifting strategies: gifting down, gifting up, qualified charitable distribution (QCD), donor-advised fund (DAF), and second-to-die life insurance policy.

GIFTING DOWN TO KIDS

You can give up to $18,000 per person per year (adjusted annually, as of 2024). This straightforward method helps distribute assets without tax consequences for the giver or receiver.

Note on pretax accounts: Under the SECURE Act of 2020, non-spouse beneficiaries must deplete inherited IRA assets within ten years, rather than spreading the tax burden over their lifetime.

GIFTING UP

This lesser-known strategy involves gifting appreciated assets, like stock, to an older relative. When passed along, the assets receive a step-up in basis, eliminating capital gains taxes. However, once given, the assets belong to them and can be used for expenses like long-term care.

QUALIFIED CHARITABLE DISTRIBUTION

For individuals aged seventy and a half or older, a QCD allows part of the required minimum distribution (RMD) to be donated to charity, avoiding taxes on the donated amount. This strategy became popular after the 2018 tax cuts, which increased the standard deduction and made itemizing deductions harder.

DONOR-ADVISED FUND

A DAF lets you donate up to 60 percent of your adjusted gross income to charity and receive an immediate tax deduction. You can also donate appreciated stocks without paying capital gains taxes, maximizing the tax benefits. Most major custodians like Fidelity or Charles Schwab offer DAFs.

LIFE INSURANCE (SECOND-TO-DIE POLICY)

For couples, a second-to-die life insurance policy is an effective way to ensure a designated beneficiary receives an inheritance after both policyholders pass away. This allows the couple to spend their remaining assets while preserving a legacy for their heirs.

FLORIDA LADY BIRD DEED/ ENHANCED LIFE ESTATE DEED

A Florida Lady Bird Deed, also known as an Enhanced Life Estate Deed, is a legal instrument that allows property owners to transfer their property to beneficiaries upon their death while retaining control over the property during their lifetime. This type of deed is particularly popular in Florida for estate planning because it avoids probate and offers flexibility and control to the grantor.

KEY FEATURES

Retained Control:

- The property owner retains full control and ownership of the property during their lifetime. They can sell, mortgage, or otherwise manage the property without needing the permission of the beneficiaries.

Avoidance of Probate:

- Upon the death of the property owner, the property automatically transfers to the named beneficiaries without going through the probate process, saving time and money.

Medicaid Planning:

- The transfer of property via a Lady Bird Deed does not count as a gift under Medicaid rules. Therefore, it does not affect the property owner's eligibility for Medicaid benefits.

No Gift Tax:

- Because the deed transfers the property only upon death, it is not considered a completed gift during the property owner's lifetime, thus avoiding potential gift tax implications.

Revocable:

- The property owner can revoke the deed at any time, retaining complete control over the property and the ability to change the beneficiaries.

Example Scenario

Consider a property owner named Jane, who wants to ensure her home goes to her children upon her death without going through probate. She can use a Lady Bird Deed to name her children as beneficiaries. During her lifetime, Jane retains full control over the property and can make any decisions regarding it. After Jane's death, the property automatically transfers to her children, bypassing probate.

STEPS TO CREATE A FLORIDA LADY BIRD DEED

Consult an Attorney:

- It is advisable to consult with an estate planning attorney to ensure that a Lady Bird Deed is appropriate for your situation and to draft the deed correctly.

Draft the Deed:

- The deed must include specific language that grants the property owner an enhanced life estate with the right to sell, convey, mortgage, or otherwise manage the property without the consent of the remainder beneficiaries.

Sign and Notarize:

- The deed must be signed by the property owner in the presence of a notary public.

Record the Deed:

- The signed and notarized deed should be recorded with the county recorder's office in the county where the property is located.

Advantages:

- Avoids Probate: Simplifies the transfer process after death.
- Maintains Control: The grantor retains the right to manage the property.
- Medicaid Planning: Does not count as a gift for Medicaid purposes.

Disadvantages:

- Complexity: Requires careful drafting and legal assistance.
- Limited Use: Not suitable for all estate planning scenarios.

REST IN PEACE

Legacy planning ensures that your money and assets are distributed in the way that you would want them. This entire process takes a couple of hours, and it prevents your beneficiaries from spending years trying to figure it all out on their own. Most people want to spare their families years in probate courts contesting a will or letting a judge decide where assets should go (with a big chunk of that given to a lawyer).

The goal of legacy planning is to give you confidence that your assets will be distributed as you intend—that you leave a legacy for your spouse, children, other loved ones, and charitable organizations. You never know when your last day will be, so take the time now to identify your beneficiaries and check your lists twice.

We've made it through the five steps of *The Better Retirement Journey*™—income, investment, tax, healthcare, and legacy planning. Now it's time to put this plan to the test and check for blind spots.

CHAPTER 8

STRESS-TESTING

Jack and Martha were several years away from retirement. They had a written roadmap in place, with a ton of Social Security planning to account for several hundreds of thousands of dollars in lifelong benefits. They had five more years of work before their retirement journey would begin at age sixty-five.

Then Congress passed the Bipartisan Budget Act of 2015, essentially closing the loopholes and eliminating the strategies that ensured Jack and Martha wouldn't run out of money during retirement. These laws changed overnight, and we had to quickly revisit their plan, make adjustments, and come up with a new strategy.

"Based on these changes, you won't have as much guaranteed income," I told them. "It'll be better for you to work an extra two years."

Their disappointment was visible.

"You don't have to work an additional two years," I said. "If everything goes perfectly, you should still be fine. But if you live a long time, do you want to risk running out of money?"

In the end, they chose to work an additional two years. They were also incredibly appreciative of the honest advice and the ability to be flexible in order to create a plan that would account for other surprises along the way.

ILLUMINATING BLIND SPOTS

When it comes to retirement, we all want to have a plan in place. And—whether they've read this book or not—most people do plan in some way, shape, or form. However, most people also make their plan assuming that their life will be normal, average, and uneventful. Most people don't account for unexpected stressors—government policy shifts, living longer than expected, losing a spouse, economies crashing, interest rates skyrocketing. Yes, their plans will work—as long as everything goes as planned.

But as Mike Tyson said, "Everyone has a plan until they get punched in the mouth."

Some of the stories you've read throughout this book show good retirement intentions going awry, with unexpected turns of events leading to shock, stress, panic, and fear. This isn't how it has to be. You can set yourself up for success by following *The Better Retirement Journey*™. You'll be ready to face unexpected challenges without fear or panic since your plan will expect the unexpected with measures in place to protect your retirement "just in case."

Let's revisit a few of the common obstacles that we've addressed along the way:

BLIND SPOT #1: BAD ECONOMY

Take the year 2000: Leroy was heavily invested in stocks and equities and had just started taking distributions. Then the market took a turn for the worse and stayed down for several years. It wasn't looking good for Leroy. As he continued to pull money, the market remained negative. The unfortunate state of the economy completely derailed his plan.

This doesn't have to be you. By using the bucketing strategy we discussed in Chapter 3—dividing your portfolio into safety, income, and growth buckets—you can maintain a diverse portfolio that weathers market fluctuations. Even if stocks are down, this strategy can help you avoid withdrawing money from volatile investments.

BLIND SPOT #2: RETIREMENT TIMING

You can't actually time your retirement to coincide with a guaranteed great economy, but you can take a look at historical returns and see how, with the bucketing strategy in place, your investments would hold up in various economic circumstances. We want to make sure that your plan works, whether you retire in a year like 2000 when the economy crashed, or in a year like 2009 when the market was on an upward climb.

The idea behind the bucketing strategy is to avoid that initial downfall. If your plan doesn't work in a year like 2000, then you should probably adjust your strategy. The bucket strategy has a volatility buffer built in—meaning, if and when the market takes a downward turn, you still have plenty of time for it to go back up. If your investments align with your own personal risk tolerance and capacity, then even in the worst-case scenario, you won't panic and move all of your assets to cash, only to miss out on subsequent capital growth.

Markets go up and markets go down. (In reality, markets are up about 76 percent of the time and down only around 24 percent. When they're higher, they're usually up by 20 percent; when they're lower, they're only down by 10 percent.) These ebbs and flows are normal (and ultimately work in your favor): sometimes it's not about timing the market as much as it's about time in the market, allowing assets to appreciate. It's a matter of being patient, letting your buckets do exactly what they're supposed to do.

A note to those prone to panic: if your monthly statements or what you hear on the news causes stress and anxiety, don't consume yourself with these things. You don't have to look at them at all. What you hear on the news is sensationalized in an effort to attract more viewers and sell more advertising dollars. Their goal is to scare you, to manipulate you into continuing to watch. Don't let this exaggerated information determine your choices.

BLIND SPOT #3: BAD ADVICE

One of my former clients called me up one day during the height of the COVID-19 pandemic. She was terrified.

"Keith, did you know that there are tunnels underneath Washington that lead to Alaska?"

This was a woman with a several-million-dollars portfolio who had been quite far from a conspiracy theorist just months prior. Now, she was convinced that these "tunnels" were part of a bigger plot to take down America.

"No," I said. "I was not aware of this."

"You have to see these videos," she told me.

She had been sucked into a rabbit hole of newsreels that were neither truthful nor helpful. She also sent me a video about how the dinar (Iraq's currency) was going to be worth a lot of money down the road. In fact, she abruptly moved to 100 percent cash in order to buy a bunch of dinar because she believed that there would soon be a repricing of all the currencies. I tried to convince her that this plan had a low probability of success, that there was no guarantee that she would make the rate of return she was hoping for.

"Historically, currencies have never fluctuated like that," I assured her.

"Well, no," she insisted. "The dinar is going to turn 10,000 percent, Keith."

We eventually had to part ways.

There's a lot of bad information and bad advice out there. It comes in the form of emails, videos, newsletters, social media, you name it. Before you take the bait, consider where this information is coming from—is this source or this person selling you something (like a newsletter or a subscription)? What's their motive? Do they want something from you (like your personal information that they can turn around and sell to someone else)?

Anytime you're getting advice, even from someone who calls themselves a financial planner, check their background. Check their credentials. You wouldn't have someone come work on your stove or washing machine who didn't have the proper qualifications to fix it. The same goes with your money—before taking any advice, know who's dishing it out. If that person isn't a CERTIFIED FINANCIAL PLANNER®—a CFP® who has gone through rigorous training and is held to a high fiduciary standard—you may want to seriously consider finding a new guide.

BLIND SPOT #4: LONGEVITY

"What am I going to do?" Eva asked me. "I just got back from the doctor and she said I'm in great shape. She said I should probably live another ten-plus years. But I'm almost out of money! What should I do?"

Now, I could tell Eva to quit being so active and eating so healthy, but aside from purposely sabotaging her health, what's this eighty-five-year-old supposed to do?

Longevity is hard to plan for. No one knows how long they'll live, and most people hardly want to consider the idea of living past one hundred. Retirement is twenty, thirty, maybe even forty years of unemployment. While only 1 percent of the population celebrates triple digits, we still want a plan in place that takes living well past seventy-five into consideration, a plan that guarantees our income will last as long as we do.

That's why *The Better Retirement Journey*™ focuses on income, rather than assets. And diverse income, at that. We want to make sure that most of your income is from guaranteed sources. Having 100 percent of your money invested in stocks or equities isn't a foolproof plan. That plan falls apart when the longevity risk kicks in. However, if you have money coming in from an IRA, Social Security, a pension, rental income, annuity distributions, and dividends, you're more protected and diversified. Even if you spend down all of your other assets because of some unforeseen circumstances, you still have a guaranteed income as long as there is breath in your body.

BLIND SPOT #5: DEATH OF A SPOUSE

I ran into Harry at the grocery store several weeks ago. I knew him from church, as a volunteer in the children's area. He knew I was in the financial business and he asked if he could speak with me for a minute. He told me that his wife had gotten sick, that they had depleted their retirement funds to pay for her care, and that she had recently passed away.

"All I have left is my Social Security," he told me. "I'm working two part-time jobs just to make ends meet." Harry is eighty-three years old.

When you're well into your eighties and have depleted your retirement savings, your financial moves are limited. Harry knew this. We mapped out a structured budget that will at least allow for some leisure activities, but unfortunately there's not a ton he can do at this stage of the game. If Harry gets sick or requires long-term care, he'll need Medicaid or he'll have to move in with one of his children who live across the country. The truth is that a few moves prior to retirement would have mitigated all these risks for Harry.

Will your plan work if your spouse dies? We've talked about this at great length—from Social Security to long-term care to beneficiary lines. If you haven't already, run the scenario. Crunch the numbers. You won't know there's a problem unless you actually stress-test the strategy and see what happens if one of you were to pass first. Then you can put a plan in place to mitigate these reductions in income—life insurance, maximizing Social Security income, and creating an income floor.

BLIND SPOT #6: LEGISLATION CHANGES

The biggest legislation risks, when it comes to your retirement financial plan, are taxes and interest rates. As we discussed in Chapter 5, we shouldn't naively hope for our government to suddenly tighten up their spending and majorly cut taxes. Instead, we should plan for higher taxes, knowing that this is a likely trajectory for our future. That's why we diversify our tax buckets and convert taxable dollars into a tax-free account. Using this method, we can offset the risk of higher taxes in the future.

THE EBB AND FLOW

Governments change policies, interest rates fluctuate, economies rise and fall, people get sick and pass away, and unforeseen events transpire. Things will happen in the next twenty or thirty years that will be alarming. This is a guarantee. But rest assured, things will also go back to normal. They always do. So, as we expect these changes and surprises to arise, it's important that our plan can change with it, that it can endure and adapt with every turn.

And, ultimately, that you can make life happen, despite these challenges. They're no longer blind spots if you can see them coming.

Another important part of the process is revisiting your plan, remembering that it's malleable and that you can make changes as needed. We encourage you to review your entire plan at least once a year, just to make sure everything is on track. This can be a quick check-in with your spouse, financial advisor, or yourself. Run through a few questions:

- Has our retirement vision changed?
- Do we need to make any shifts?
- Do we have any concerns?

Brace yourself for things looking and feeling different than you anticipated. Especially in the first year, things do often change. Maybe travel isn't as enjoyable as expected. Maybe you decide you want to travel more. Maybe additional concerns or considerations arise that you need to take into account. Remember—this is the norm, not something to stress about.

Take the time to revisit the plan and, if there are significant changes, map it out again.

If you've followed *The Better Retirement Journey*™, stress-tested your plan, and committed to the process, then you're ready for the best part of the plan: making life happen. Get out there and enjoy retirement—go on that trip to Africa, buy that house in the mountains, spend time with your grandchildren, play a hundred rounds of golf, and soak up all of these moments. You've earned it.

CONCLUSION

Joe and Betty were in a great financial situation, with plans to fully retire in the near future. After twenty years working for an engineering firm, Joe had a nice pension lined up. Betty had stepped away from her full-time job as a nurse a few years prior due to health issues.

They sat across from me in my office and Joe asked, "How should we handle my pension? Should we choose 100, 50, or 0 percent? We're leaning toward zero."

"Why?" I asked.

Joe went on to explain that Betty was a recent cancer survivor and a few years older than him. Based on her struggling health, they both thought it was far more likely that Joe would outlive Betty, and the bigger monthly pension check was appealing. They were fairly certain they would need the income to cover their monthly expenses.

I couldn't help but be reminded of my grandmother's bleak financial situation after we lost my grandpa. I would never want anyone else to experience the hardship that she had to face. But I had more than just an anecdotal story to tell—I was armed with *The Better Retirement Journey*™ process.

I assured Joe that 0 percent survivorship was a valid option and something to seriously consider. But there were also several risks involved. Rather than tell Joe what these risks were, I showed him.

We walked through the process together and created a written plan for Joe and Betty, outlining all possibilities, including 0 percent survivorship in the unfortunate event that Joe predeceased Betty. We used a Monte Carlo simulation to assess the plan's viability. A Monte Carlo simulation is a statistical method that runs thousands of scenarios to predict the likelihood of different outcomes based on various market conditions and other variables.

On paper, when we set the survivorship to 0 percent and had Joe pass early in retirement, Joe could see that the likelihood of success for their initial plan was less than 10 percent, which depended on near-perfect market conditions and everything aligning ideally. However, when we adjusted the survivorship percentage to 100, the Monte Carlo simulation showed that the likelihood of the plan working in various scenarios skyrocketed to 95 percent.

I asked Joe, "Do you love your wife?"

He said, "Well, yes, of course I do."

I explained, "God forbid, if something unrelated to your health happens to you—you get in a car accident or fall off a cliff—with the 0 percent survivorship plan, Betty is going to be left destitute."

When Joe was able to see the numbers in writing, to see the impact his original plan would have had on his beloved wife in the worst-case scenario, Joe changed his mind. He wanted to ensure that his wife was taken care of, no matter the circumstances. That was far more important than an additional $600 a month from his pension.

A few months later, Betty called to tell me that Joe had suffered a massive heart attack and passed away. She was sobbing. We were deeply sorry for her loss and we scheduled time for her to come in to discuss her finances and next steps.

After a big hug, Betty looked up at me with tears in her eyes and said, "Am I going to be okay?"

Thanks to *The Better Retirement Journey*™ process we went through, and the scenarios we meticulously tested, documented, and discussed, I could confidently assure Betty that, from a financial standpoint, she would be fine. This allowed her to grieve the loss of her husband without worrying about her financial future.

Joe never thought that Betty would outlive him; it was difficult for him to discuss and imagine her being left behind. But if it weren't for this conversation and seeing actual numbers on paper, Betty's life would have looked much different these past ten years. She would have had to go back to work or—more likely—move in with her daughter, son-in-law, and their three young children. She would be stressed about income and, instead of focusing on her own wellness and healing, she would be focused on surviving. Just getting by. Certainly not the vision of retirement either of them had.

But walking through *The Better Retirement Journey*™ changed both their perspectives. It allowed Joe and Betty to make informed decisions based on many possibilities that matched their picture of the future. And Betty has been able to pick up the pieces and continue to live a fulfilling life in retirement.

Betty's story was the exact opposite of my grandmother's. It is for situations like these that we created this plan to ensure that our clients can fully embrace and enjoy retirement, and that they are taken care of when the worst-case scenario becomes reality.

TAKE ACTION

Now that you've completed the planning process, it's time to do something with it.

Take Tammy and Todd as inspiration. They went through *The Better Retirement Journey*™ with us at our office a few years ago. In our vision-casting meeting, they both lamented that their parents had always talked about all of the trips they wanted to take in retirement, but they never got around to it. Tammy and Todd were both concerned that this was what retirement was about—dreaming but never *doing*.

We spent several weeks mapping out their plan and putting everything in place. They had their Top Ten List, income and investment streams lined up, and long-term care, tax, health-care, and legacy plans in place. By the end of our planning process, it was clear to both of them that they could take all of the trips on their list. And what's more—there was no reason to wait. We had barely finalized all the details when they told me they booked a European cruise—for the following week!

"There's no better time than right now," Tammy said. "We're ready to start this journey."

I hope you feel the same way—ready to start this journey off on the right foot. I hope you're holding your own plan in your hand right now. Or that it's sitting next to you on your kitchen table. Or that you've framed a copy and hung it on your wall to remind you of what's to come. Because hopefully this journey has brought you peace of mind, confidence, and excitement for the days and months and years ahead.

You see, you only get one shot at retirement, and there aren't any do-overs. That's why we truly believe you should step into retirement like you would a multiday hiking trip—with a map, a sturdy pack, the proper gear, food and water, and the skills and knowledge to adapt, pivot, and thrive (and a satellite phone, in case of emergency). You put the time and effort in on the front end so that you can enjoy the adventure undistracted by the what-ifs or taken out by the unexpected.

Now, you can take a deep breath. You've done the hard work. While you can't control the future or foresee all that life will bring your way, you can rest assured that you are holding the ticket to the retirement you have dreamed of. But now what?

If you haven't done the worksheets, go back and do them. Put pen to paper and crunch your numbers. This is how you know that your plan will work.

If you've completed all of the worksheets, take the next step—adjust your investments, book a trip, put money into a Roth account or an asset-based long-term healthcare plan. Identify a few action items and check them off your list.

If you have a financial advisor that you like and trust, call this person up, schedule a meeting, and enlist their services to help implement all you've written down. If you don't have one, use cfp.net to find a local CERTIFIED FINANCIAL PLAN-NER® to be sure they are held to a fiduciary standard. Meet with that CFP® face-to-face and get busy.

The plan won't work if you don't put it into place—the sooner you can implement, the better. And remember, none of this is set in stone. Don't be afraid to make changes (in fact, please do make changes, especially if something big happens). Return to your plan and check back in once a year to make sure you're still on the right track, and make adjustments as needed. Life will change and your plan should change with it.

MAKE LIFE HAPPEN

In our office media room—where we host our podcast—we have a digital wall with a big neon sign that says MAKE LIFE HAPPEN. On this wall are pictures our clients have sent of their retirement adventures—Gary and Beth at the Grand Canyon, Brendon and Letitia on a sailboat off St. Thomas, Adam and Laura scuba diving in the Maldives. These are people, just like you, who have walked through *The Better Retirement Journey*™ process and are enjoying the other side. They're soaking up the freedom, knowing that they can enjoy every moment, without financial stress, anxiety, or fear.

My hope is that you would join this wall of friends, people who are out there making the most of their retirement because they can. And you can too. With *The Better Retirement Journey*™ plan in place, you can live out your dreams, trusting that the plan has you covered. You can step into your new retirement life with confidence, hope, and peace of mind.

It's time to make life happen. Send us your pictures when you do!